MONDAY, JUNE 16

Fresh M...
1 ¾ cups min...
2 tablespoons lem...
Green food color...
3½ cups (1½ lbs) ...
½ bottle ...

National Bank

WASHINGTON CATHEDRAL

WASHINGTON, DC 20016

T SAINT ALBAN

THE TWENTY-SECOND SUNDAY AFTER PENTECOST
22 OCTOBER 1972

MORNING PRAYER AND SERMON AT ELEVEN

Services for Trial Use, First Order
Page numbers refer to the Book of Common Prayer.
The peoples' parts are in italic capitals.

langsam (Sonata 3)   Paul Hindemith

YMN 513

Lord in the beauty of holiness:
WHOLE EARTH TREMBLE BEFORE HIM.

SIN

MOST MERCIFUL FATHER, WE HAVE ERRED
FROM THY WAYS LIKE LOST SHEEP. WE
TOO MUCH THE DEVICES AND DESIRES
EARTS. WE HAVE OFFENDED AGAINST THY
WE HAVE LEFT UNDONE THOSE THINGS
IT TO HAVE DONE; AND WE HAVE DONE
WHICH WE OUGHT NOT TO HAVE DONE.
ORD, HAVE MERCY UPON US; SPARE
O CONFESS THEIR FAULTS; RESTORE
O ARE PENITENT; ACCORDING TO THY
ARED UNTO MANKIND IN JESUS CHRIST
GRANT THAT HEREAFTER WE MAY LIVE
TEOUS AND SOBER LIFE, TO THE GLORY
AME. AMEN.

Following the absolution, all stand.

Salad Cranberry Salad

1 T gelatin
3 T cold water
1 pkg lemon jello
1 tart apple   1 C pecans

Deep South Staples

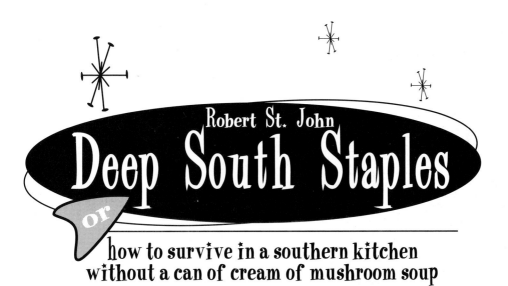

Robert St. John

Deep South Staples

or

how to survive in a southern kitchen
without a can of cream of mushroom soup

HYPERION

New York

Library of Congress Cataloging-in-Publication

St. John, Robert
Deep South staples, or, How to survive in a southern kitchen without
a can of cream of mushroom soup / Robert St. John.
p. cm.
Includes index.
ISBN 1-4013-0838-4
1. Cookery, American—Southern style. I. Tile.

TX715.2.S68S6625 2006
641.5975—dc22
2005052603

Hyperion books are available for special promotions and premiums.
For details contact Michael Rentas, Manager, Inventory and Premium Sales,
Hyperion, 77 West 66th Street, 11th floor, New York, New York 10023,
or call 212-456-0133.

FIRST EDITION

1 3 5 7 9 10 8 6 4 2

*For Jill, Holleman, and Harrison
in remembrance of family meals shared
and in anticipation of family meals to come*

Contents

Foreword

I have been watching Robert St. John since his mama made him hush and be still in the sanctuary of the Main Street Methodist Church in Hattiesburg, Mississippi. When Mrs. St. John walked down the aisle with her two blond-headed boys in tow, my grandmamma would lean over and whisper, "Just look at those St. John boys . . . aren't they sweet?"

Although I was forced to live ninety miles up the road in the state capital of Jackson, Hattiesburg, the home of my beloved grandparents, Hiram and Helen Todd, is the magical place that holds the sweetest of my memories. My people knew Robert St. John's people. They prayed together, banked together, bought lady peas from the same vendor at the Curb Market, and their lives were inexorably threaded together in the intricate social fabric of small town Southern life.

Robert St. John grew up to become a chef and successful restaurateur but he was born to be a writer. He was blessed with the gift of being able to cook it and to write about it. Like the best of true cooks, Robert has hospitality in his heart, but more important, he understands the meaning and the deeper significance of the traditional foods on the Southern table. His insightful essays reveal that this is a man who knows that every Southern woman is judged by the quality of her biscuits and that the best sweet tea is found in states with two teams in the Southeastern Conference.

Robert wrote this book, *Deep South Staples,* for me, for my own mama, and for all of us who weren't paying attention while the peas were being shelled, the okra was being fried, and the biscuits were being made. I've been cooking all my adult life—mostly exotic dishes with difficult-to-pronounce names that require imported and expensive ingredients and tools. Sadly, I don't have a clue about how to make the foods I dream about, the foods that hold memories for me such as pot roast, fried green tomatoes, and banana pudding. I can get out my trusty wok and whip up a dish of Mongolian Beef in no time . . . but the

thought of chicken and dumplings fills me with fear. And don't even mention biscuits . . . or fried chicken!

Frying a chicken has become a symbol for me and for my mother of all the things we forgot to learn or were too busy to learn from the one true cook in our family, my grandmother. We miss her Thanksgiving dressing, her biscuits, fig preserves, and red velvet cake. We love to talk about the way she magically whipped up a pound cake on what seemed like a moment's notice. And we long for that sound of Sunday fried chicken sizzling and popping in the cast-iron skillet on the stove. My grandmother wanted to teach us, and offered to teach us, but we always laughed and said, "We'd just rather you cook it for us." We thought we had all the time in the world.

I am grateful that Robert St. John took the time and was paying attention, bless his heart. He was paying attention in his grandmother's kitchen and in the kitchens of his Hattiesburg, Mississippi, neighborhood where he rode his bike from house to house in search of his "second supper." Even as a small child, he was discriminating between houses where TV dinners were served and those where the real cooking was done.

Robert's book is seasoned with both recipes and stories that celebrate our Southern past, but he has updated these hand-me-down recipes for the twenty-first century. All of the recipes—even the chicken and dumplings—are easily prepared and made with ingredients found at your local grocery store. Cream of mushroom soup has been ceremoniously and lovingly replaced with a tasty mushroom béchamel sauce. Time moves on, and ingredients change, but the importance of cooking for our family and friends is unchanged.

Food matters. Tradition matters. And the community recipes that bind us one to another like the patchworks on an old quilt matter. Robert St. John has handed down the cast-iron skillet from one generation to the next.

Somehow, there is order in the universe and the heavens are smiling, because Mrs. St. John's grandson is teaching Mrs. Todd's granddaughter to fry a chicken and make biscuits.

Carol Todd Puckett Daily
June 21, 2003

Preface

The South excelled in two things which the French deem essential to civilization: a code of manners and a native cuisine. – John Peale Bishop

My friend Sarah Webb is an excellent cook. I have dined in her home often. She reads *Bon Appétit, Food & Wine,* and *Gourmet* religiously. The foods I have enjoyed in her home are of that cooking style. Four years ago, I ran into Sarah at the Hattiesburg Farmer's Market. With a somewhat puzzled look on her face, she approached me, a pint of pink-eye purple-hull peas in hand, and said, "What do I do with these?"

I was baffled. Certainly someone with Sarah's extensive cooking prowess would know what to do with a simple pint of peas. I quickly told her how to make a stock using ham hocks which could also be used for butter beans or turnip greens, and she was on her way.

My encounter with Sarah lingered in the back of my mind for the next few weeks as I continued to have similar, chance meetings with other good cooks. That is, good cooks who could do amazing things with angel-hair pasta, smoked salmon, boutique herbs, micro greens, and paté, but were at a loss when it came to making a chicken pot pie. These cooks were using complicated procedures to prepare the hip and trendy foods-of-the-moment, but had no idea of how to prepare creamed corn and fried chicken—the foods of our grandmothers, soul food, Southern food, comfort food, heritage food.

I myself had been a victim of this strange phenomenon years earlier. I was in my twenties before a housekeeper showed me how to fry chicken. At the time, my restaurant, the Purple Parrot Café, had been open for a couple of years. I had made my bones developing sophisticated restaurant dishes using complicated, professional cooking techniques. All this, and I couldn't fry chicken worth a damn.

For many years, Southern cooks have dumped a can of peas into a pot, thrown in a slice of bacon, added a pinch of salt, and summoned everyone to dinner. In restaurants, vegetables are often cooked

in a stock. Whereas a Southern cook will throw a ham hock into salted water with turnip greens, a restaurant chef will make a stock using ham hocks, reduce it to intensify the flavors, and then use that liquid to cook the greens. That is what we have done in this book.

It's a no-brainer: Take a few classic, time-proven restaurant techniques and put them into practice in the home kitchen—nothing complicated, no foreign, hard-to-find ingredients, no complex methods or procedures, just honest home cooking with readily available ingredients, updated and legitimized for the home cook.

A few years ago, I jotted down seven cookbook concepts on a sheet of paper. I then ranked them in the order I wanted to write them. The book that eventually became *A Southern Palate* was first on the list. Second on the list was this book. Although I was raised on home cooking and I love home cooking, I went through a ten-year stage of my life when I ate almost nothing but fine-dining food. I emerged from that stage looking forward to simpler cuisines, foods that were familiar, foods that reminded me of loved ones and good times long gone. As a matter of fact, I am still in that stage and plan to be for the rest of my life. Restaurants are my profession; eating is my passion.

The problem with a lot of Southern cooking is the ever present can of cream of mushroom soup. It, along with the microwave, has been the downfall of our native cuisine. Food in the Deep South is a religion. I grew up Methodist. We Methodists eat a lot. I have attended many a covered-dish supper that offered green bean casseroles made with cream of mushroom soup, broccoli casseroles made with cream of mushroom soup, chicken casseroles made with cream of mushroom soup, and even soups made with cream of mushroom soup. This book is a departure from that style of cooking, but it is not a departure from the ideas and tastes that inspired it. The dishes are all here; they just taste better.

I developed the list of recipes for this book with the help of my friend and culinary mentor, Mary Virginia McKenzie. After the initial list was created, I sat down with Purple Parrot Café's chef de cuisine and recipe tester, Linda Nance, to map out a game plan. Linda grew up in California. The foods of her youth and the foods of my youth are sometimes diametrically opposed. After I familiarized her with the ways of the Southern kitchen,

the fun began. We discussed the traditional preparations of the Deep South staples I grew up eating and how I wanted to update them. I taught Linda about pink-eye purple-hull peas, hoppin' John, and chicken pie and she showed me the finer points of developing a rich and flavorful tomato sauce.

The first recipe out of the chute had to be a replacement for the omnipresent cream of mushroom soup. We bought a can of grocery store soup and dumped it onto a plate. A large, gray, gelatinous form, still in the shape of a soup can, lay before us. We knew it wouldn't be hard to improve on this mess. Within two days, we had produced a replacement that was, hands down, worthy of any Southern kitchen. After that, it was full speed ahead.

With some dishes, Linda took the ball and ran with it. The meat loaf recipe in this book is entirely hers and it will turn any non–meat loaf eater (such as me) into a raving fan. Macaroni and cheese was a dish I had never eaten, not even as a kid. Linda volunteered her recipe, we tweaked it once, and it worked out great. I have always loved the French toast she prepares for the Purple Parrot Café's Sunday brunch. I made sure that it, too, was included. Dishes such as green

bean casserole and spinach Madeleine were ones I had grown up eating. They are among the group that have been updated and legitimized for this book, along with a variety of Southern vegetables and a few of the casseroles that I cook at home.

One of the recipes that took the longest to develop happened to be one of the easiest. For years, I have tried to recreate my grandmother's biscuits, to no avail. She served them at every dinner she ever hosted. I loved them. They were small and light and I could eat them by the basketful. She served them on her fine china for Thanksgiving lunches and Christmas Eve dinners and she served them on her everyday china for breakfast. She never used a recipe while preparing her biscuits, and I never took the time to ask her to write one down. Today, I am eating lesser biscuits for it. We have come close to her recipe in this book with the Sunday Dinner Biscuits recipe on page 197.

With all this righteous talk of scratch biscuits I must awkwardly admit one of my deepest, darkest culinary guilty pleasures—I am an in-the-closet Jiffy corn bread junkie. When I was growing up my mother made Jiffy often. It was cheap to buy and easy to make. South-

ern cooking purists will scoff at the notion of boxed corn bread. Lewis Grizzard would scold the Southern cook who served corn bread containing sugar. I like it; so as far as I'm concerned, the purists can take a hike. Lewis Grizzard is long dead, so give me Yankee Corn Bread (recipe page 202) any day. The purists can revel in the fact that they won't be buying prepackaged, premixed corn bread and others can prepare the basic corn bread recipe—sans sugar—on page 201.

There are many traditionally Southern recipes that are not included in this book, some because I didn't have room and others because I don't like eating or cooking them. Even though they were the preferred salad at every formal Sunday lunch of my youth, I have not included any type of congealed mold or aspic. Also, I am proud to say that there isn't a recipe for tomato-flavored gelatin topped with mayonnaise nor are there any with JELL-O and store-bought whipped cream. There are no desserts that make use of instant pudding and you won't find sweet potatoes topped with marshmallows or anything that uses any type of soup—mushroom or not—as a base for any of these recipes. There is definitely not a recipe for carrot salad anywhere in sight. As a matter of fact, my contract with bookstores requires that no book with a carrot salad recipe be allowed within three feet of this book (a culinary restraining order if you will).

Naturally, Southerners' eating habits have changed over the years. However, change at the expense of good taste and fond memories is tragic. These recipes are not laws chiseled in stone. They are open to improvisation—if you are lacking one ingredient, use your imagination and substitute another. The main objective is to have fun.

I gained twenty-five pounds testing these recipes. Not necessarily because the foods are more fattening than others, but because they taste so good. I went back for seconds, thirds, and sometimes fourths. I could eat the banana pudding and meatloaf recipes in this book on a daily basis.

For years, I have collected cookbooks and recipes. There are books in my collection that are over a hundred years old. I have secret recipes passed down from restaurant friends and recipes given to me by loyal readers of my newspaper column. The most valued recipes and books in my collection belonged to my grandmothers and great-grandmothers. They were written on the back of old cancelled checks and notepads, detailed procedures noted on the backs of garden-club programs and bridge-club scorecards, and five-course menus written on bits and pieces of old calendars and phone books. My grandmother Eunice St. John was the original recipe collector in the family. She was an excellent cook and loved to talk food with friends, old and new. In researching this book, I found a recipe for a congealed cranberry salad that was written on the back of a church bulletin from the National Cathedral in Washington, D.C. I imagine she was visiting her son (my uncle) in Alexandria, Virginia, met a lady at church, and then, on the steps afterward, traded recipes before she even got off the church property.

The essays in this book are reworked from my weekly food column. They are stories of friends and family and the South. The common vein that runs through all of the stories is food—restaurant food, house food, good food, bad food, strange food—it doesn't matter. We encounter them all in the everyday life of the Deep South. The essays tell of the things that Southerners, and I among them, hold dear, the Four F's: Faith, Family, Friends, and Food. To me, these are the most important things in life, and whenever anyone can combine all four in one setting, the memories that are created are magical.

This is not only a book for you, the reader, but a book for me and my family. Halfway through the recipe-testing phase of this book, I turned to my wife and said, "I didn't set out to do this, but I think I have created the go-to guide for home cooking at the St. John house." This book will be the one we use when we cook Thanksgiving lunches, Christmas Eve dinners, school-night suppers, Friday night cocktail parties, or just plain old snacks. I hope the reader derives as much use from *Deep South Staples* as I plan to.

Sarah is now cooking peas like a pro. If you spend a little time with this book, cooking the recipes listed within, you will be, too. Now stop reading this preface and get to cooking!

Photo and Illustration Credits

Acknowledgments

Thanks to:

Linda Nance, Purple Parrot Café chef de cuisine—for tireless help with recipe testing, recipe development, and recipe creation, and for producing the best damn meat loaf recipe on the planet! Not too shabby for an expatriate Californian.

Jill, best friend, best wife, best mother, and biggest fan—for being a sounding board and my rock.

John Langston, book producer extraordinaire—for publishing knowledge and patience.

Denton Gibbes, book designer, promoter, marketing guru, and possum catcher—for many things, not the least of which is a major-league last-minute bailout.

Wade Rico, graphic designer—for working under the gun.

Geoff Pender, pre-edit editor and essay proofreader—for five years of copy editing, wasting dozens of red pens, and Christmas Eve sofa chuckles.

Nell Smith, Bettee Boyd, and **Steve Barthelme**—for fostering creativity, believing in the underdog, and working with the long shot.

Mary Virginia McKenzie, Southern cooking consultant, friend, neighbor, and recipe contributor—for being a constant source of inspiration.

Bill Kirby, friend, writer, raconteur—for physically beating the preface out of me.

Stacey Andrews, marketing ace and salesperson-of-the-century—for being a right hand on the back end.

Clint Taylor, friend, business partner, and Purple Parrot Café general manager—for holding down the fort.

Shane Stanford, friend, counselor, and checker champion—for inspiration and examples.

Wyatt Waters, friend, advisor, and fellow music aficionado—for constant advice and support.

Nick Apostle, friend, chef, mentor, and teacher—for giving me my start.

John Evans, bookseller, counselor, and enthusiastic supporter—for wise counsel.

Cathy Creel, typist and secretary—for keeping it all straight.

Maria Keyes, bookkeeper—for handling the cabbage (or lack thereof).

Recipe contributors: **Muz** (pancakes), **Mom** (green bean casserole), **Mam Maw** (chicken salad, bridal pudding), **Joan Holland** (banana pudding), **Barbara Jane Foote** (tea), **Larry Foote** (pecans), **Louis Norman** (pickles), **Gene Saucier** (slaw).

Sixteen years' worth of restaurant customers, column readers, and television viewers without whom none of this could have been possible.

xvii

Deep South Staples

Cocktail Party Fare

Cheese Straws

Warm Seafood Dip

Sausage Cheese Dip

Mexican Sauce

Southwestern Dip

Larry Foote's Salty
Cocktail Pecans

Deviled Eggs

Boiled Shrimp

Cheese Straws

½ cup	Butter, unsalted
½ lb	Sharp cheddar cheese, shredded
1¾ cups	Flour
1 tsp	Cayenne pepper
2 tsp	Worcestershire sauce

Preheat oven to 300 degrees.

Place butter and cheese in the container of a food processor. Add flour, cayenne, and Worcestershire and blend thoroughly. If you don't use a food processor, knead by hand or use an electric mixer with a paddle attachment. Shape dough into a ball and roll out on a lightly floured surface to ⅛ inch thick. Use a knife to cut strips about ½ inch wide and 5 inches long.

Place on a baking sheet lined with parchment paper and bake for 20–25 minutes. Rotate pan after 10 minutes. Cool and serve.

Yield: 5 dozen

Cooking Tips

Storing Olive Oil

Olive oil should be stored at 57 degrees (the same temperature as a wine cellar) in a tightly covered container.

Heat, light, and air will eventually cause your oil to go rancid.

Cloudy olive oil usually means it has gotten too cold.

Once it has warmed up, it will clear up.

Warm Seafood Dip

2 Tbl	Light olive oil
½ lb	Shrimp, 60–70 count, fresh, rough chopped
2 Tbl	Onion, minced
1 Tbl	Garlic, minced
1 Tbl	Green bell pepper, minced
2 tsp	**Creole Seasoning (recipe page 252)**
2 tsp	Salt
2 tsp	Hot sauce
¼ cup	Half-and-half
½ lb	Crab claw meat
½ lb	Cream cheese, softened
4 oz	Velveeta, cut into cubes
4 oz	Sharp cheddar cheese, shredded
1 Tbl	Lemon juice, fresh

Heat olive oil in a large skillet over high heat. Add shrimp and cook 4–5 minutes. Add onion, garlic, and bell pepper and continue to cook 2–3 more minutes. Add Creole seasoning, salt, hot sauce, and half-and-half. Bring to a simmer, reduce heat to low, and add remaining ingredients. Using a wooden spoon or a rubber spatula, stir the mixture until cheeses are melted. Stir in the lemon juice. Serve immediately.

Yield: 8 servings

Sausage Cheese Dip

1 lb	Spicy breakfast sausage
2 Tbl	Garlic, minced
2 Tbl	Onion, small dice
2 Tbl	Bell pepper, small dice
2 tsp	Hot sauce
1 tsp	Salt
1 lb	Cream cheese, softened

In a large skillet brown the sausage. Drain the grease and add garlic, onion, and bell pepper. Continue to cook 3–4 minutes. Place sausage into a mixing bowl and, while still hot, add remaining ingredients. Use an electric mixer and mix until everything is well incorporated. Serve warm with chips, French bread, or your favorite crackers.

Yield: 8 servings

Mexican Sauce

15-oz can	Ro Tel tomatoes
1 cup	Tomato sauce
1 Tbl	White vinegar
2 tsp	Cumin
2 tsp	Jalapeño slices, minced
1 tsp	Garlic powder
1 tsp	Salt
1 tsp	Black pepper

Combine all ingredients in a small sauce pot. Simmer 4 minutes on low. Remove from heat and allow mixture to cool for 10 minutes. Place in a blender and purée until smooth. If you want to increase heat, add more minced jalapeños. Use as a dip with chips or as a topping for burritos and enchiladas.

Yield: 2½ cups

Southwestern Dip

1 cup	Sour cream
1 cup	**Mexican Sauce (recipe page 6)**
¼ cup	Cilantro, chopped
½ cup	Green onion, chopped
1 Tbl	Lime juice, fresh
1 tsp	Salt

Combine all ingredients and mix well. Serve chilled.

Yield: 2 cups

Cooking Tips

Making Extra Counter Space

A quick way to make temporary counter space in a small kitchen is to use the ironing board, which provides about four extra feet for cooling dishes or for bowls and utensils as you work.

Funeral Food

Funerals are observed in many different ways.

Military funerals embrace the playing of "Taps" and the firing of rifles. In New Orleans, an old-fashioned jazz funeral becomes a festive Mardi Gras parade once the body has been buried. In the movies, Irish mourners hold a wake and get knee-walking drunk while singing "Danny Boy" (the Italians go for red wine and "Ave Maria").

In the South, we eat.

Down here, our response to a death is so Pavlovian that, as soon as a death is mentioned, our first thought is, "Who is going to make the potato salad?" Before we think of the grieving widow or the loss of a friend, we are wondering if anyone else is going to bring deviled eggs. In the South, a wake means fried chicken, egg salad, and cream of mushroom soup–filled casseroles.

Southern ladies band together after a death. It is amazing to see. Out of instinct, love, tradition, honor, and a desire to bake, they rally around the cause to take care of their own and feed the masses.

The food at these events is plentiful. Not only does the bereaved

family have to shop for a casket, they must go to the appliance store and buy a new freezer to hold the massive quantities of green bean casserole, corn pudding, chicken salad, yeast rolls, brownies, and coconut cakes that have been delivered to their doorstep.

My hometown of Hattiesburg used to have a drive-through funeral home. No kidding. The funeral home was open and running in the late 1970s. There was a huge, horizontal plate-glass window on the side of the building. The funeral home would place a casket in the window and mourners would drive alongside to view the body. We called it "The Moan and Drive-on."

The drive-through funeral home eventually closed, probably because no food was available. Realizing they were located in the Deep South, they should have put a service window on the other side of the building and handed mourners squash casserole and vegetable crudités with a side of fries and a large Coke on their way to see poor old Uncle Harry. "Doesn't he look natural, James? I feel sorry for Helen and the kids. Please pass the asparagus . . . and slow this car down!"

My grandmother brought elaborate dishes to the homes of the bereaved. She went to work as soon as she heard of a death in the community. A favorite dish she prepared on such occasions was bridal pudding. I'll never know why she took a wedding dessert to a funeral, but it obviously worked. People still talk about it.

The dish was delivered to the house in three parts to be composed later. That is a lot of work for both parties. Times were different then. Grandmothers were different then. My grandmother was different, too. She was one of the most gracious and socially adept people I have ever known. Her visits to the hospital to comfort sick friends took half a day. This is the same lady who, at eighty-seven years old, had a heart attack, but drove herself to the beauty parlor to have her hair done before driving herself to the emergency room.

In the South, death and food are synonymous. Down here, communities band together in times of tragedy. Food is the common vein that runs through us all. However, my generation doesn't seem to come together as those generations before us did. Are we so busy that we have forgotten the importance of community, friends, and family?

As a child, I attended my share of funerals. There was always a mountain of food available. Those early funerals probably played a big part in my love for Southern food (and also in my girth). A lot of my friends are chefs and restaurateurs. If you want some good food, come over to my house when I kick the bucket. But don't hold your breath.

Mothers make us go to funerals. Wives make us go to weddings. Dads take us to football games. In the South, we eat at all three.

Larry Foote's
Salty Cocktail Pecans

1½ lbs   Pecans, whole
Unsalted butter, to taste (cut into 1 Tbl pats)
Salt, to taste

Preheat oven to 320 degrees.

Place pecans in a 13 x 9 aluminum baking pan with 2-inch sides. Dot with 5 pats of butter and lightly salt the pecans. Place in oven for 10 minutes. Remove pan from oven and gently fold (stir) in pecans with a wooden spoon, adding 3 pats of butter and a light sprinkling of salt. Repeat this cooking procedure every 10 minutes, slightly increasing the amount of salt each time, while lightly decreasing the amount of butter. Never add more butter than the pecans can absorb in a 10-minute period, and be very gentle when stirring the pecans.

The entire process takes 60–65 minutes. When done, spread a layer of pecans on wax paper and dig in.

Yield: 1½ pounds

Deviled Eggs

1 dozen	Eggs, hard-boiled, peeled, and cut in half
2 tsp	White balsamic vinegar
⅓ cup	Mayonnaise
¼ cup	Sour cream
1½ tsp	Salt
2 Tbl	Yellow mustard
Pinch	White pepper
⅛ tsp	Garlic, granulated

Paprika and sweet pickle relish to garnish (optional)

Remove the yolks from the hard-boiled eggs and place in a mixing bowl. Set the egg whites aside. Add all remaining ingredients and beat with an electric mixer until smooth. Use a pastry bag to fill the egg whites. Sprinkle with paprika and place a tiny amount of sweet pickle relish on the eggs.

Yield: 24 halves

Cooking Tips

Deviled Eggs

In order to avoid deviled eggs that are too large for the mouth, use the smallest eggs possible; then, after boiling, cut a nickel-size slice from each end to stabilize them.

Halve the eggs crosswise, not lengthwise, to make them small enough to eat gracefully.

Boiled Shrimp

3 qts	Water
3 Tbl	Crab boil, powdered
2	Bay leaves
2	Lemons, halved
2 Tbl	Salt
1 Tbl	Black peppercorns, whole
2 lbs	Shrimp, large and unpeeled

Place all ingredients except the shrimp in a large sauce pot and bring to a boil. Turn heat down so the mixture comes to a fast simmer. Continue to boil for 20 minutes. Place the shrimp in the simmering liquid and set a timer for eight minutes. Remove and drain shrimp. Spread on a cookie sheet and place in refrigerator to cool. Or eat right away

Yield: 6–8 servings

Breakfast Foods

Muz's Pancakes

Breakfast Casserole 1

Breakfast Casserole 2

Perfect Scrambled Eggs

Egg-in-the-Hole

Eggs Benedict

Garlic Cheese Grits

Grillades and Grits

Mary Virginia's Orange
Sweet Rolls

Bananas Foster French Toast

Amaretto-Brûlée

Breakfast Bread

Linda's French Toast

Muz's Pancakes
(The World's Best)

1 cup	Flour, all-purpose
2 tsp	Baking powder
1 tsp	Baking soda
½ tsp	Salt
1 Tbl	Sugar
1	Egg
1 cup	Buttermilk
½ cup	Melted butter, divided

Mix dry ingredients thoroughly. Gently add liquid ingredients, including ¼ cup of butter, and stir until just incorporated. Do not overwork the batter. The batter is thick; if you like, it can be thinned with a small amount of water or a little more buttermilk.

Cook pancakes on a lightly greased griddle. Pancakes should be turned only once. They are ready to be turned when bubbles form in the middle and the edges appear cooked. Once pancakes are turned, use a pastry brush to spread the additional melted butter on top of the pancakes while the other side is cooking. This will keep you from having to spread cold butter on them, which will tear them. The pancakes will already be buttered once they reach the table. Top with real maple syrup.

Pancakes

A good way to keep pancakes warm without them becoming soggy is to cover them with an inverted colander.

Breakfast Casserole 1

1 lb	Spicy breakfast sausage
¾ cup	Onion, diced
¼ cup	Green bell pepper, sliced
¼ cup	Red bell pepper, sliced
1 tsp	Garlic, minced
1 tsp	**Creole Seasoning (recipe page 252)**
1 tsp	Cayenne pepper
10	Eggs, beaten
1 cup	Half-and-half
1 tsp	Dry mustard
¼ cup	Butter, softened
6 pieces	White bread, crusts removed
6 pieces	Wheat bread, crusts removed
1 cup	Sharp cheddar, shredded
1 cup	Monterey jack cheese, shredded
1 tsp	Hot sauce

Preheat oven to 325 degrees.

Brown sausage in a large skillet and drain most of the fat. Add vegetables, garlic, and seasoning and cook 5 minutes. Set aside.

Mix together eggs, half-and-half, and dry mustard in a mixing bowl. Using the softened butter, butter both

sides of each slice of bread. Cut the bread into small cubes. Fold the bread, cheeses, sausage mixture, and hot sauce into the eggs. Mix well and place in a buttered 2-quart baking dish.

Bake for 40–50 minutes. Allow to rest 15 minutes before serving.

Yield: 8 servings

Bacon Fat

You should never throw away bacon fat.

If you need to dispose of a small quantity, line a coffee mug with tin foil and pour it in.

When the fat hardens, pull out the foil and toss it in the trash can, never in the sink.

Breakfast Casserole 2

1 lb	Bacon, thick-sliced, diced
2 cups	Onion, diced
1 cup	Red bell pepper, diced
1 Tbl	Garlic, minced
5 oz	Spinach, frozen, thawed and dried well
10	Eggs, beaten
1 cup	Half-and-half
1 tsp	Worcestershire sauce
1 tsp	Dry mustard
1 tsp	Salt
1 tsp	**Creole Seasoning (recipe page 252)**
1 tsp	Black pepper
½ cup	Butter, softened
6 slices	White bread, crusts removed
6 slices	Wheat bread, crusts removed
2 cups	Swiss cheese, shredded

Preheat oven to 325 degrees.

In a large skillet, cook bacon until it begins to brown; drain excess fat. Add onion and continue to cook until onion begins to brown. Add red pepper, garlic, and spinach, and cook 2 more minutes. Set aside.

In a mixing bowl, combine, eggs, half-and-half, and

seasoning. Spread the softened butter on both sides of each slice of bread. Cut the buttered bread into small cubes. Combine all ingredients, add cheese, and mix well.

Place in a buttered 2-quart baking dish. Bake for 40–50 minutes. Remove from oven and let rest 15 minutes before serving.

Yield: 8 servings

Sweet Tea

When asking for iced tea in a restaurant, Southerners say "tea, please." We mean sweet tea. The sweet is always implied. If we want unsweetened tea, we ask for it.

Sweet tea is steeped in tradition. It's a Southern thing. My rule for finding restaurants that serve sweet tea is easy: If the state doesn't include a member of the Southeastern Football Conference, you will have a hard time finding sweet tea (the two exceptions being East Texas and parts of North Carolina). States with two teams each in the Southeastern Conference—Mississippi, Alabama, and Tennessee—make the best sweet tea.

Tea gets sweeter as you travel deeper into the South. That rule works for women, too.

Our restaurants serve more than two hundred gallons of iced tea a week, three-quarters of which is sweet. Some Southern restaurants don't serve sweet tea. I was once a waiter at a restaurant that didn't serve sweet tea. There was a daily insurrection. Folks are particular about their iced tea. If it doesn't come presweetened, they will forgo tea altogether and order a Coke. Or worse, ice water.

I don't order tea in Chinese restaurants. They might do a good job with hot tea, but I have never had a memorable glass of iced tea in a

Chinese restaurant. Some restaurants, in an effort to save money, try to save their tea overnight. Any restaurant worth its tea leaves will always dump unused tea down the drain and start fresh the next day.

Some people drink instant iced tea. I have never tasted an instant tea that was any good. It always tastes like tea-flavored Kool-Aid. How hard can it be to boil water and steep a few bags? There are many boutique teas that come in various shaped bottles at local grocery stores and convenience stores. I don't like them either.

I hate sun tea. It's a scam. I imagine sun tea drinkers also are dog beaters and jaywalkers. Sun tea is weak. In the 1970s, my mother (who is not a dog beater) bought a glass gallon jar with the words "Sun Tea" printed on the outside. There was nothing unique or unusual about this container. Set it in the sun, watch it brew. Wow! The same guy who invented the Pet Rock invented the sun tea jar. He was definitely a dog beater.

Some folks add a pinch of baking soda to their tea while it is steeping. They claim that this removes the bitterness and makes the color richer. I say, buy a good quality tea and you won't have to worry about bitterness. Steep it long enough and you won't have to worry about color.

My grandmother put a sprig of mint in her tea. Once, while serving lunch to a man who was painting her house, the painter said, "Mrs. St. John, there is a leaf in my tea!"

Not wanting to embarrass him, and in her usual, gracious manner, she replied, "Oh, I am sorry, if you don't like it, you may remove it."

My grandmother made great tea. She always kept iced tea in washed-out mayonnaise jars in her refrigerator. She learned how to make her version of iced tea from an English gentleman. My uncle, her son, came home from Harvard for a weekend visit. He brought his roommate, an English fellow named Roger P. R. Bennett. Bennett gave my grandmother the secret to making great tea. She claimed that the Brits knew how to make tea better than anyone.

I remember the day my grandmother told me the ancient British secret to her tea-making process, but I don't remember the actual secret. It wasn't anything extraordinary, just a little twist in the procedure. Like many other things she showed me in the kitchen, I didn't write it down. Now I am old and forgetful and I am drinking lesser tea for it. My favorite iced tea is served at the Windsor Court Hotel in New Orleans. At the Windsor Court, they do not serve sweet tea. However, they serve simple syrup along with their iced tea. Windsor Court is a British-inspired hotel. Maybe they know Roger P. R. Bennett's secret. I will ask.

The moral is: Don't drink tea outside the Southeastern Conference. Never order iced tea in a Chinese restaurant. Don't beat your dog for fear that someone will call you a sun tea drinker, and whenever you are in the kitchen cooking with your grandmother, take notes.

Perfect Scrambled Eggs

3	Eggs, large
2 tsp	Half-and-half
1 Tbl	Butter

Salt and pepper to taste

Crack eggs in a small bowl and stir well with a fork until the yolks and whites have just incorporated. Do not stir too vigorously or you will add air to the eggs. Add half-and-half to eggs and stir well.

In a nonstick skillet over moderately low heat, melt the butter and tilt the pan to coat the entire surface. Add the egg mixture to the skillet. Using a rubber spatula, slowly scrape the bottom of the skillet until the eggs begin to coagulate. Continue to stir the eggs carefully until they are "just done." The eggs should be almost fully cooked and custard-like (Julia Child calls them "custardy lumps") yet have a slight sheen to them.

Remove eggs from the skillet immediately and transfer to a plate (the eggs will continue to cook slightly for the next 30–45 seconds, so it is imperative to remove them just before they are done). Add salt and pepper to taste.

Yield: 1–2 servings

Egg-in-the-Hole

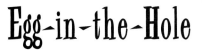

1 slice	Whole wheat sandwich bread
1 Tbl	Unsalted butter
1	Egg (medium or large)

Salt and pepper to taste

Using a cookie cutter, cut a hole in the center of the bread slice. Place butter in a nonstick skillet over medium to medium-high heat. Once butter begins to foam, add bread slice and sauté (not moving the bread) for 20 seconds. Gently press down the sides of bread so that it is sitting flat on the pan. If the bread is moving up and down due to the sizzling butter, the heat is too high.

Crack an egg into the center of the bread slice. Cook approximately 1 minute. Very carefully, flip the bread using a spatula large enough to cover the entire piece of bread. Cook on other side for approximately 1–2 minutes to desired doneness (over easy is best).

Transfer to a plate and season with salt and pepper.

Yield: 1 serving

27

Cooking Tips

Eggs

To find out whether an egg is fresh or not, immerse it in a pan of cool salted water.

If it sinks, it is fresh.

If it rises to the surface, throw it away.

Eggs Benedict

1 lb	Ham, thinly shaved
8	English muffins, split
2 tsp	White vinegar
16	Eggs

Salt and pepper, to taste
Hollandaise Sauce (recipe page 29)
Parsley, freshly chopped for garnish

Brown ham in a medium skillet.

Toast the English muffins, cut sides up, on a baking sheet under the broiler.

Fill a 10-inch nonstick skillet ½ full of water. Add white vinegar to the cooking water. Bring to a slow boil. Gently crack 1 egg into the water, taking care not to break the yolk. Reduce heat to a gentle simmer. Cook 3½ minutes or until the egg white is set and yolk remains soft. Remove with a slotted spoon, allowing the water to drain off the egg. Repeat process with remaining eggs.

To assemble: Lay 1 ounce of shaved ham on top of each muffin half, followed by a poached egg. Season with salt and pepper. Spoon hollandaise sauce over egg. Garnish with chopped parsley.

Yield: 16 servings

Hollandaise Sauce

8	Egg yolks
2 Tbl	Lemon juice, freshly squeezed
1 Tbl	White wine
2 sticks	Unsalted butter, melted
Dash	Hot sauce
1 tsp	Salt

Vigorously whisk egg yolks and lemon juice together in a stainless steel bowl until the mixture is thickened and doubled in volume. Place the bowl over a saucepan containing simmering water (the water should not touch the bottom of the bowl). Continue to whisk rapidly. Don't let the eggs get too hot or they will scramble. Slowly drizzle in melted butter and continue to whisk until the sauce is thickened and doubled in volume.

Remove from heat, whisk in hot sauce and salt. Cover and place in a warm spot until ready to use. Can be made 30 minutes in advance. If the sauce gets too thick, whisk in a few drops of warm water before serving.

Jill's Green Egg Pellets

Julia Child once told me that most people underestimate the importance of being able to properly cook a scrambled egg.

Over a memorable breakfast, Child and I discussed egg scrambling methods and techniques. My wife was sitting at the table, but she obviously wasn't paying attention.

My wife cannot scramble eggs.

The first time I ate my wife's scrambled eggs was during the first breakfast she ever cooked for me. It was early in our marriage and the eggs arrived at the table tinted an unusual blue-green hue. I thought the odd color might be coming from a renegade ray of light beaming through the breakfast room window, reflecting off the wallpaper and onto my plate. No such luck. The eggs were green. Not wanting to disrupt the bliss that is newlyweddedness, I remained silent (and hungry).

After a few months and a dozen more helpings of uneaten breakfasts, she asked me why I didn't like scrambled eggs anymore.

In a weak and reckless moment, I blurted out that the problem wasn't scrambled eggs in general, but her scrambled eggs (In those days I was young, stupid, and unwise in the diplomatic ways of a harmonious marriage). The old proverb states, "Eggs cannot be unscrambled." Likewise, comments about your wife's scrambled eggs cannot be retracted and I was left with egg on my face.

Ah, yes, breakfast at the St. Johns'.

Actually, my wife's eggs are not as much scrambled as they are rubbery, green egg pellets. Wasn't there a 1970s Top 40 hit called "God Didn't Make Little Green Rubbery Egg Pellets"? Obviously, long before the good Lord and AM radio found out about my wife's cooking.

I don't know the exact chemical process that occurs to make an egg turn green, but my wife has discovered it. No, she has perfected it. It is sort of like Easter in reverse. Instead of the shell being dyed, it's the yolk and whites (make that greens) that are colored. I imagine that my wife will one day be lecturing all of the great chemistry minds at Harvard, MIT, and Jones County Junior College on this amazing sautéed chicken embryo–tinting process.

In addition to being green, their texture is remarkably rubbery.

Simply transferring a plate of my wife's scrambled eggs from the kitchen to the breakfast room is an adventure; they haphazardly roll around on the plate. When walking with a plateful of my wife's rubbery, green egg pellets, one must be careful to keep the plate level at all times lest the eggs roll off the plate, fall onto the floor, and bounce back into the kitchen, at which time you must return to the kitchen, pick up the pellets, and start the process all over again. My wife is the only person I know whose breakfasts require delivery tips and walking instructions.

My wife likes cheese in her eggs. The correct way to add cheese to eggs is to sprinkle finely grated cheese over the top just as the eggs are removed from the skillet. If cheese is added during cooking, the oil in the cheese will be released and the finished product will be oily.

Why do her eggs turn green? First off, they are overcooked. Second, she adds pepper during the cooking process. Third, she doesn't care what I think about her eggs. She likes them overcooked, hard, and cheesy and has let me know as much, often (as I'm sure she will do after she reads this).

Maybe it is because she uses Pam cooking spray instead of butter. Pam is useful for some types of cooking, but the only "nonstick" that should grace a scrambled egg skillet is butter. Eggs, salt, pepper, a touch of cream, and butter, that's it. No Pam.

> I will not eat green eggs with Pam.
> I will not eat them, Rob I am.
> I will not eat them if they bounce.
> I will not eat them, not an ounce.
> I will not eat those eggs of green.
> I will not eat discolored cuisine.
> I will not eat them; do I have to yell it?
> I will not eat those green egg pellets.

For the record (and because I like sleeping in my own bed), my wife cooks excellent pancakes and never once in her illustrious flapjack-flipping career have her pancakes come out green or rubbery.

Garlic Cheese Grits

1 Tbl	Bacon grease or oil
1 Tbl	Garlic, minced
1 tsp	Salt
2 cups	Milk
2 cups	Chicken broth
1 cup	Grits
1 tsp	**Creole Seasoning (recipe page 252)**
1 tsp	Hot sauce
8 oz	Sharp cheddar cheese, shredded
4 oz	Cream cheese

Melt bacon grease over low heat in a 1½ quart sauce pot. Add garlic and salt and cook for 1–2 minutes, being careful not to brown the garlic. Add milk and broth and increase heat. Bring to a simmer and slowly pour in the grits. Lower heat and cook grits for 15 minutes, stirring often.

Add remaining ingredients and stir until cheeses are melted. Serve immediately.

Yield: 8 servings

Grillades and Grits

½ cup	Bacon grease (or canola oil)
2 lbs	Veal top round cut into 2-inch strips
1 Tbl	Black pepper, freshly ground
2 tsp	Kosher salt
¾ cup	Flour
¾ cup	Onion, diced
¼ cup	Shallot, minced
½ cup	Celery, diced
¾ cup	Green bell pepper, diced
½ tsp	Dried thyme
1 tsp	Garlic, minced
3 cups	Chicken broth, hot
½ cup	Red wine
1	Bay leaf
1 cup	Tomatoes, peeled, large dice
2 tsp	Hot sauce
1 tsp	Salt

Place 1–2 tablespoons of the bacon grease in a large heavy skillet and place on high heat. Season meat with 1 teaspoon of the freshly ground pepper and the kosher salt. Place the meat in hot skillet. Once browned, remove meat from the skillet.

Place the remainder of the bacon grease into skillet. Once melted, lower heat and slowly stir in flour. Cook 3–4 minutes. Add onion, shallot, celery, peppers, thyme, and garlic. Continue to cook roux mixture for 4–5 minutes. Using a wire whip, stir in the hot chicken

broth, red wine, bay leaf, and tomatoes and bring to a simmer.

Add veal back to the mixture and cook over very low heat for 2–3 hours, stirring occasionally. When meat is tender, stir in hot sauce, the remaining black pepper, and salt.

Prepare garlic cheese grits during the last 30 minutes of cooking. Spoon grits onto a serving dish and top with grillades.

Yield: 8 servings

Mary Virginia's Orange Sweet Rolls

1 stick	Butter
1 batch	**Icebox Roll Dough (recipe page 200)**
1¼ cups	Granulated sugar
1½ Tbl	Cinnamon
1 lb	Confectioner's sugar

Grated rind of two navel oranges
Enough orange juice to make a glaze

Using melted butter, grease 6 aluminum foil–lined 9-inch cake pans.

Roll out Icebox Roll dough into a large rectangle (1 foot x 3 feet). Sprinkle with granulated sugar and cinnamon.

Roll up dough, jellyroll style, from the long side. Cut ¾-inch-thick slices and place into prepared cake pans. Let rise until doubled in size (about 1 hour).

Bake in a preheated oven at 350 degrees for 15 minutes.

Make a glaze using confectioner's sugar, orange rind, and orange juice. Ice rolls while they are hot. These rolls freeze well in Ziploc bags, but if you are like me, they won't last long enough to make it to the freezer.

Yield: Not enough

Pour Easily

To get heavy, sticky liquids to pour out of measuring cups easily, rub the inside with corn oil.

Bananas Foster French Toast

Batter

6	Eggs
2 cups	Half-and-half
½ cup	Sugar
2 tsp	Cinnamon
2 tsp	Orange zest, fresh
1 tsp	Vanilla
1 stick	Butter

1 large loaf of French bread, sliced on a diagonal into 1½-inch-thick pieces

1 pat butter for frying

Bananas Foster Sauce

1 stick	Butter
4 cups	Bananas, sliced
¾ cup	Pecan pieces
1½ cups	Butter pecan or maple syrup
2 Tbl	Dark rum

Preheat oven to 200 degrees.

Combine all ingredients for batter and stir well. Soak French bread slices in batter for 5 minutes. Heat butter over medium heat in a large skillet. Brown the soaked bread on each side and place in a baking dish. Keep French toast in the oven to keep warm until all slices have been cooked.

To make the sauce, add butter and bananas to the same pan. Cook for 4–5 minutes and add the rum. Allow alcohol to burn off. Stir in the pecans and syrup. Remove French toast from oven and top with Bananas Foster sauce. Serve immediately.

Yield: 6–8 servings

Dining with the Banshee

Some parents stop dining out after their children are born.

For most of my life that baffled me. I used to naively proclaim, "The only way children are going to learn how to act in restaurants is to take them to eat in restaurants." And I meant it.

I wrote columns about how restaurants should be more kid-friendly. "Parents are growing tired of fast food," I would say. "Take your children to full-service restaurants. Bite the bullet and teach them good restaurant manners." And I believed it.

My daughter had always been the perfect restaurant customer. She was dining at Windsor Court and Emeril's when she was nine months old. She was neat, quiet, well-behaved, and sweet. . . . She still is.

My wife and I didn't alter our lifestyle one iota after our daughter was born. We traveled to the same cities, ate in the same restaurants, and stayed in the same hotels. Life was good. Things were calm. The three of us lived a quiet, peaceful, and civilized existence.

And then came the boy.

My son is not a good restaurant customer.

Don't get me wrong; he is a happy boy. He is so happy that he screams for no reason. As a matter of fact, he screams often and for no reason. Actually, when he's in a restaurant, he screams constantly and loudly for no reason. He has such an intense passion for food that he wails like a banshee if you don't feed him fast enough, using the proper procedure.

This feeding procedure is very complicated and not well suited for restaurants. It takes multiple spoons, a lot of space, and the combined efforts of at least two highly skilled and thoroughly trained professionals—one to feed the boy, the other to quickly load the second spoon for the next bite. We have found that the "auxiliary-spoon method" (sometimes called the "steady-shovel method") works best. However, once a bite has been taken, one must be in position and ready with the next bite or the Yoko Ono–inspired banshee wailing session begins.

The boy doesn't chew as much as he inhales. I had always heard of someone "inhaling" food, but I had never actually seen it happen until he came along. Trust me; it's not a pretty sight.

He may be rowdy, but he is plenty smart. Actually, he is brilliant, and will one day be offered dozens of scholarships to numerous Ivy League institutions. In a Nobel-worthy breakthrough, he has already discovered a way to absorb food into his digestive system by smearing it into his cheeks, eyes, ears, and hair. This new method of food assimilation through the epidermis is sure to be the subject of many laboratory reports in the distant future.

Why does he smear food all over his face? I don't know. Maybe it has something to do with his intense detestation of toilet paper. My one-year-old son is on a personal crusade to rid the world of all toilet paper. It is his life's mission. If a roll of toilet paper can be found in any bathroom, he will be there to unravel it and drag it through the house, restaurant, or store. His world will not be safe until he has emptied every toilet paper roll in existence.

After twenty-two years in the restaurant business, I thought I had seen it all, from toddlers dancing on tables to kindergarteners throwing salad plates across the dining room like Frisbees. Now my karma has caught up with me.

When our daughter was an infant, my wife and I would sit in restaurants and pity the parents of rowdy and out-of-control kids. From our high-and-mighty perch in well-behaved-babyland, we would pompously whisper, "We are such good parents. Look at how well-mannered our child is. Those other parents just don't know how it is done. If only they would ask us for advice, we could give them the answer." As we reached around to pat ourselves on the back, I imagine we were already writing the introduction and dedication to the "How to Be a Good Parent" manual.

We were wrong; very, very, very, very wrong. It occurred to me the other day as I was chasing my son through a restaurant (someone else's restaurant, mind you . . . Daddy is smart, too). He had escaped my grasp and was making a break for parts unknown.

I ran past a couple sitting in a booth with their well-behaved child, their only child. They had that look on their faces. I knew the look. It used to be my look. It was the look of "We know how to raise a well-behaved baby. That man has no clue." The look had come back to haunt me from another life. A quieter life. A less frantic life. A well-behaved life.

I stopped running and took a seat, a defeated man. But then I was hit with a jarring bolt of enlightenment. And as I watched my son head-butt the hostess stand, two things became crystal clear. One: He must be a result of his mother's gene pool. Two: That couple has another thing coming the next time around. They'll get theirs.

Holding a Bowl Steady

To keep a bowl steady when whisking with one hand and pouring with the other, place the mixing bowl on a wet kitchen towel to hold it in place.

Amaretto-Brûlée Breakfast Bread

⅓ cup	Butter, melted
¾ cup	Brown sugar
2 Tbl	Honey
2 Tbl	Pecans, chopped (optional)
2 Tbl	Almonds, slivered and blanched (optional)
8	French bread croutons, cut into 1-inch-thick rounds
4	Eggs
⅔ cup	Milk
¼ cup	Heavy cream
⅛ tsp	Cinnamon
⅛ tsp	Nutmeg
1 Tbl	Vanilla
1 Tbl	Amaretto
	Powdered sugar for dusting

French bread croutons should be cut out of a baguette-style French bread loaf. Slices should be 1 inch thick.

In a cast-iron skillet, combine butter, brown sugar, and honey over medium-high heat. Cook mixture, stirring constantly until bubbly and sugar has dissolved. Add nuts. Pour Brûlée into the bottom of a round, 2-quart Pyrex baking dish. Allow Brûlée to cool slightly, then top with the French bread croutons.

In a large mixing bowl whisk eggs, milk, heavy cream, cinnamon, nutmeg, vanilla, and Amaretto. Pour mixture evenly over the croutons. Using the tips of your fingers, press bread down gently to force custard into croutons without breaking. Cover dish with plastic wrap and refrigerate overnight.

Preheat oven to 350 degrees.

Allow custard to come to room temperature 1 hour before baking. Bake uncovered until French bread is puffed and edges of croutons are golden brown (approximately 40 minutes). Place a plate on top of the baking dish. Using dish towels or pot holders, invert dish onto a plate. Top with powdered sugar.

Yield: 4–6 servings

Linda's French Toast

Filling

2 lbs	Cream cheese, softened
1 Tbl	Orange zest
¾ cup	Sugar
2 tsp	Vanilla
1½ tsp	Cinnamon

Batter

2 cups	Half-and-half
2 cups	Milk
8	Eggs and 4 yolks
1 tsp	Vanilla
¾ cup	Sugar
1 tsp	Cinnamon
½ tsp	Nutmeg

French bread, cut into 8 pieces, 5 inches long each

To make the filling, mix all ingredients together using an electric mixer until light and fluffy. Hollow out a 1-inch tunnel through the center of the French bread pieces. Fill a pastry bag with the cream cheese filling and stuff the French bread.

Make the batter mixture and pour it over the stuffed French toast.

Let soak for 2 hours or longer. Rotate the bread often so that all sides become equally saturated.

Preheat oven to 375 degrees.

Place French toast on a well-buttered sheet pan and place in oven. Bake 12 minutes. Remove and turn bread over. Return to oven and bake 8 more minutes. Serve with warm maple syrup and fresh sliced strawberries.

Yield: 8 servings

Salads and Soups

Mam Maw's Chicken Salad

Summer Corn Salad

Smoked Turkey Salad

Tomato, Onion, and Cucumber Salad

West Indies Salad

Crawfish Potato Salad

Potato Salad

Sweet Slaw

Shrimp and Okra Gumbo

Vegetable Beef Soup

Chicken and Corn Chowder

Potato Soup

Vichyssoise

Tomato Soup

Mam Maw's Chicken Salad

2	Carrots, peeled and quartered
1	Onion, peeled and quartered
3 stalks	Celery
1	3–5 lb Chicken
	(or 5 cups cubed chicken breast)
⅔ cup	Sweet pickle relish, drained
1¼ cups	Miracle Whip
½ tsp	White pepper
1 tsp	Salt
3	Eggs, boiled and chopped
½ tsp	Garlic powder
½ tsp	Onion powder
1 cup	Celery, chopped fine

Fill a stockpot ½ full with cold water and add carrots, onion, and celery. Bring to a boil and add chicken. Return to a slow boil and cook until chicken is cooked through. Remove chicken, let cool, and chop or shred. Combine with remaining ingredients.

Yield: 1½ quarts

Cooking Tips

Preflavoring Frozen Chicken Breasts

To give skinless chicken breasts more flavor, place them in a labeled zipper lock freezer bag with your choice of marinade.

Seal the bag and place it in the freezer until ready to use.

Herbs

Hold fresh herbs by the stem and plunge them into cool water several times; shake them and pat them dry with a paper towel.

To store, place herbs (stem down) into a narrow container that will keep them upright.

Add an inch or two of cold water, wrap with plastic wrap, and refrigerate.

Summer Corn Salad

8 ears	Silverqueen corn, roasted, cut from the cob (approximately 6 cups)
1 cup	Tomato, seeded, small dice
½ cup	Red onion, minced
¾ cup	Green bell pepper, small dice
2 Tbl	Cilantro, chopped
2 Tbl	Parsley, chopped
1 tsp	Garlic, minced
1 tsp	Cayenne pepper
1	Lime, squeezed for juice
1 Tbl	Cider vinegar
1 tsp	Salt
¼ cup	Olive oil

Combine all ingredients and mix well. Refrigerate at least 1–2 hours before serving. Best when made a day ahead.

Yield: 6–8 servings

Smoked Turkey Salad

5 cups	Smoked turkey meat, loosely chopped
1 cup	Celery, chopped
½ cup	Green onions, chopped
3 Tbl	Parsley, chopped
1 Tbl	**Creole Seasoning (recipe page 252)**
½ cup	Sliced almonds, toasted lightly
11 oz can	Mandarin oranges, drained

Combine all in a mixing bowl and add just enough dressing to bind the ingredients. Any additional dressing can be used for chicken or tuna salad.

Yield: 2 quarts

Smoked Turkey Salad Dressing

1½ cups	Hellmann's mayonnaise
1 Tbl	Worcestershire sauce
1 Tbl	Hot sauce
1½ tsp	Salt
1 Tbl	Paprika
1 Tbl	Balsamic vinegar
1 tsp	Horseradish
1 tsp	Dijon mustard

Combine all ingredients together.

53

Cooking Tips

Cutting Boards

If a cutting board doesn't have a reservoir to collect the meat juices, place the board in a lipped cookie sheet or sheet pan and carve as usual.

Tomato, Onion, and Cucumber Salad

½ tsp	Garlic, minced
¼ cup	Red wine vinegar
1 tsp	Dried basil
½ tsp	Black pepper, freshly ground
1 Tbl	Orange juice
¾ cup	Olive oil
1 tsp	Salt
3 cups	Ripe tomatoes, peeled, seeded, and diced
¾ cup	Vidalia onion, thinly sliced
1½ cups	Cucumbers, peeled, seeded, and cubed

Combine the first 7 ingredients and mix well. Toss with the vegetables and refrigerate. Chill for 3 hours before serving. Best if made a day ahead.

Yield: 6–8 servings

West Indies Salad

1 lb	Crabmeat, jumbo lump
½ cup	Red onion, chopped fine
¼ cup	Canola oil
¼ cup	White vinegar
1 Tbl	Parsley
1 Tbl	Hot sauce
2 tsp	Worcestershire sauce
1 tsp	Salt
½ tsp	Black pepper

Gently combine all ingredients and refrigerate overnight. Serve on sliced tomatoes, on a bed of lettuce, or as an appetizer with crackers.

Yield: 4–6 servings

Cooking Tips

Vidalia Onions

Because of the high sugar content, Vidalia onions spoil easily; always store them so that they are not touching each other.

Crawfish Potato Salad

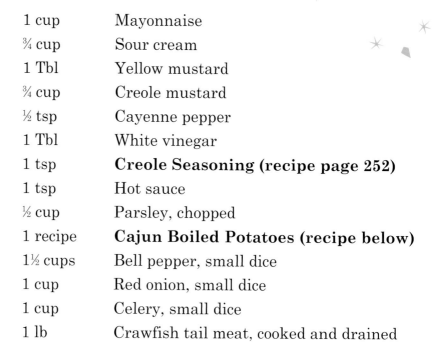

1 cup	Mayonnaise
¾ cup	Sour cream
1 Tbl	Yellow mustard
¾ cup	Creole mustard
½ tsp	Cayenne pepper
1 Tbl	White vinegar
1 tsp	**Creole Seasoning (recipe page 252)**
1 tsp	Hot sauce
½ cup	Parsley, chopped
1 recipe	**Cajun Boiled Potatoes (recipe below)**
1½ cups	Bell pepper, small dice
1 cup	Red onion, small dice
1 cup	Celery, small dice
1 lb	Crawfish tail meat, cooked and drained

Combine the first 9 ingredients and mix well to form the potato salad dressing. Add cooked potatoes and the remaining ingredients and mix well.

Yield: 2 quarts

Cajun Boiled Potatoes

6 cups	Red new potatoes, quartered, skin on
2 Tbl	Crab boil (powder form)

| 1 tsp | Salt |
| 3 quarts | Water |

Place potatoes, crab boil, and salt in the water and simmer on low heat until potatoes are tender. Drain and allow the potatoes to cool.

57

Potato Salad

6 cups	Idaho potatoes, peeled and cut into a large dice
3 quarts	Water
2 tsp	Salt

Place potatoes and salt in water and simmer on low heat until potatoes are tender. Drain and allow to cool.

2 cups	Mayonnaise
½ cup	Yellow mustard
1 Tbl	Dijon mustard
2 Tbl	Cider vinegar
1 tsp	White pepper
1½ tsp	Black pepper, freshly ground
2 tsp	Salt
1 cup	Green onion, chopped
1 cup	Red bell pepper, small dice
1 cup	Celery, small dice
4	Eggs, hard-boiled and chopped
¼ cup	Sweet pickle relish

Combine the first 7 ingredients to form a dressing. Add potatoes and all other ingredients to the dressing and mix well.

Yield: 2 quarts

Vienna Sausage

What's the story behind Vienna sausages?

Do they hail from Vienna, Austria? Are people actually eating mechanically processed chicken in the foothills of the eastern Alps? In the land of strudel, schnitzel, and Sacher torte, have the locals developed an affinity for minced pork with sodium erythorbate? Was a Vienna sausage the inspiration for Beethoven's Ninth Symphony? Could the "Ode to Joy" initially have been called the "Ode to Sodium Nitrates"? Are Viennese fishermen using them for bait while fishing the Danube? Will I ever stop asking silly hypothetical questions and segue into a more meaningful and insightful essay?

Probably not, but it's my job to ponder these all-important and life-changing food issues. Besides, I've got plenty of time on my hands.

I have been to Austria. While there, I saw no one eating anything that looked like a Vienna sausage. But they do eat a lot of sausages

there. Really big sausages—morning, noon, and night. In Austria, when you order dessert, it comes with a side order of sausage.

I have never eaten a Vienna sausage (pronounced: "Vie–yen–nee" in South Mississippi). The taste of mechanically separated chicken has never been one of my frequent and recurring food cravings. According to the U.S. Department of Agriculture, mechanically separated chicken is "a paste-like poultry product produced by forcing bones with attached edible tissue through a sieve or similar device under high pressure to separate bone from the edible tissue." Yummy! Let's all pop a top.

Even if I could get past the bones-and-tissue thing, I am scared of that gelatinous goo on top of Vienna sausages. It looks like some type of slimy pork-flavored jelly.

Did you know that Vienna sausage goo is on the FBI's list of the twenty most dangerous weapons? It can be extremely dangerous. A case in point:

My friend and celebrated watercolorist, Wyatt Waters, talks of a 1964 trip his family took in the Waterses' unair-conditioned Chrysler Windsor station wagon. On the hottest day of the summer, they drove from Clinton to the Six Flags amusement park in Dallas.

From the front seat, Wyatt's mom manned the food rations. His father, Coach Waters, drove with the single-minded purpose of a we're-not-stopping-for-anything father on vacation. As Mrs. Waters handed out slices of red-rind hoop cheese and Vienna sausage to her three sons in the backseat, the coach pressed on.

Wyatt, being one who has always marched to the beat of a different drummer, was more interested in receiving relief from the summer heat than eating lunch. He spent most of the trip holding his head out of the window so the wind could blow on his face. Somewhere west of Shreveport, Louisiana, Mrs. Waters held a can of Vienna sausages out of the front window to drain the juice.

Newton's Law of Flying Sausage Goo No. 1 states: Vienna sausage slime in a hot can on a scorching day will gradually become less jelly-like and more fluid.

Newton's Law of Flying Sausage Goo No. 2 states: If one is sticking his head out of the backseat window of a fast-moving vehicle while another is draining a can of hot Vienna sausage liquid from the front seat window, the person in the backseat will inevitably receive a steaming hot face full of blistering and putrid Vienna sausage juice.

Wyatt was momentarily blinded. The juice was in his ears and up his nose. His face was red and smelly. To this day, he still claims that Brylcreem can't hold a candle to Vienna sausage jelly, as his hair was permanently slicked back in a James Dean–style sausage-goo pompadour for the rest of the day. (Wasn't there a shampoo in the seventies called "Gee, Your Hair Smells Like Mechanically Separated Chicken"? But I digress.)

Whether this incident gave Wyatt a new perspective with which to view the world as an artist, we'll never know. However, he no longer sticks his head out moving car windows in the summertime.

Sweet Slaw

1 cup	Sugar
1 cup	Mayonnaise
½ cup	White vinegar
2 Tbl	Milk
2 Tbl	Mustard, prepared
⅛ tsp	Salt
½ tsp	Celery seeds
½ tsp	Dry mustard
6–8	Peppercorns
6 cups	Cabbage, shredded
2 cups	Carrots, shredded

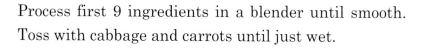

Process first 9 ingredients in a blender until smooth. Toss with cabbage and carrots until just wet.

Yield: 8 servings

Shrimp and Okra Gumbo

½ cup	Canola oil
¾ cup	Flour
3 Tbl	Filé powder
1 cup	Onion, diced
½ cup	Celery, diced
½ cup	Bell pepper, diced
1½ cups	Fresh okra, sliced
2 Tbl	Garlic, minced
1½ lbs	Shrimp, small, peeled
2 tsp	Salt
1½ tsp	Black pepper
2 tsp	**Creole Seasoning (recipe page 252)**
1½ tsp	Basil, dry
1 tsp	Thyme, dry
1 cup	Tomatoes, diced, canned or fresh
2 quarts	Shrimp stock
1 Tbl	Hot sauce
¼ tsp	Cayenne pepper

In a large skillet, combine oil, flour, and filé powder to form a roux. Cook over medium heat, stirring often until roux is very dark (be careful not to burn). Add vegetables, garlic, shrimp, and spices and continue to cook for 5–7 minutes, stirring constantly to prevent burning. Meanwhile, bring tomatoes and shrimp stock to a boil.

65

Artichokes

In order to keep artichokes upright while cooking, either sit them stem side down into the bands of canning jar lids or slice an onion into very thick slices and use the outer rings to sit the artichoke in for support.

Slowly add roux mixture to boiling stock and mix well. Lower heat to a slow simmer, and cook 10 more minutes. Add hot sauce and cayenne pepper.

Yield: 1 gallon

Vegetable Beef Soup

3 Tbl	Olive oil
1½ lbs	Beef shoulder, small dice
1½ tsp	Salt
1 tsp	Black pepper
1 cup	Onion, small dice
1 cup	Carrot, small dice
1 cup	Celery, small dice
1 Tbl	Garlic, minced
½ tsp	Dried thyme
2 tsp	**Steak Seasoning (recipe page 253)**
1	Bay leaf
15 oz can	Tomato, diced
1½ quarts	Beef broth
1 cup	V-8 juice
1 cup	Corn, fresh, scraped from the cob
1 cup	Potato, peeled and diced
1 Tbl	Worcestershire sauce
1 Tbl	Kitchen Bouquet

Heat 1 tablespoon of oil over high heat in a large skillet. Season the meat with ½ of the salt and pepper. Brown the meat in olive oil. Do not overload the skillet. Overloading the skillet will cause the beef to steam instead of brown. Brown meat in batches, add more oil when necessary, then place cooked meat in a large stockpot.

Cooking Tips

Storing Meat

The correct way to freeze cooked meat to prevent freezer burn and retain moisture and flavor is to put it in a zipper lock freezer bag, surround it with au jus, demi-glace, or gravy, and remove all air from the bag.

Add 1 tablespoon of oil to skillet and sauté the onions, carrots, celery, and garlic for 5 minutes over medium heat. Add thyme, steak seasoning, and bay leaf. Deglaze the pan by adding the canned tomatoes (with the juice) using a wooden spoon to remove any stuck-on particles. Cook 5 minutes on high, and add to the meat in the stockpot. Place beef broth in the stockpot and cook over low heat. The soup should just barely simmer. After 1 hour, add V-8, corn, and potatoes. Continue cooking another 45 minutes. Remove from heat and stir in remaining salt, pepper, Worcestershire, and Kitchen Bouquet.

Yield: 1 gallon

Chicken and Corn Chowder

¼ lb	Bacon
½ lb	Onions, small dice
1 Tbl	Black pepper, freshly ground
3 tsp	**Poultry Seasoning (recipe page 254)**
1½ cups	Chicken breast, raw, chopped
¼ cup	Flour
1 quart	Chicken stock or broth
2 cups	**Creamed Corn (recipe page 164)**
2 cups	Red new potatoes, skin on, quartered, cooked and drained
2 cups	Heavy whipping cream, hot
½ cup	Half-and-half, hot
2 Tbl	Hot sauce

Chop bacon, render, and drain fat into stockpot. Add onions and black pepper and sauté until tender (do not brown). Season chicken with poultry seasoning, add to pot, and cook through. Add flour, mixing well. Cook without browning for approximately 5 minutes. Add chicken stock slowly, stirring until smooth. Add corn. Add drained potatoes. Add hot cream, half-and-half, and hot sauce.

Yield: 1 gallon

My South II

While channel surfing the other day, I came across a clichéd program about the South. The supposed Southerners were talking about eating possum.

As long as I have lived in the South I have never eaten a possum. No one I know has ever eaten a possum. I have never been to anyone's house who served possum. I have never seen possum offered on a restaurant menu and I have never seen possum in the frozen meat section of a grocery store.

I have, however, seen possums running through the woods. And I have seen a few possums (who weren't good runners) in the middle of the road.

In the South, we might eat strange foods, but possum isn't one of them.

As far as Hollywood is concerned, the South is still one big hot and humid region full of stereotypes and clichés (they got the humidity part right). We are either Big Daddy sitting on the front porch in a seersucker suit, sweating and fanning while drinking mint juleps beside a scratching dog, or the poor barefooted child in tattered clothes, walking down a dusty dirt road beside a scratching dog. There is no middle ground. Most of the time, we are either stupid or racist or both.

The South of movies and TV, the Hollywood South, is not my South.

- In my South, no one eats possum. We do, on occasion, accidentally run over them.
- In my South, little girls wear bows in their hair.
- In my South, banana pudding is its own food group.
- My South doesn't have hoagies. In my South, we eat po boys.
- In my South, the back porches are screened and the front porches have rocking chairs and swings.
- In my South, the ham is as salty as the oysters.
- In my South, everyone waves.
- In my South, we know the difference between yams and sweet potatoes.
- In my South, we eat every part of the pig, just like they do in Paris.
- In my South, we use knives, forks, and spoons, but we let cornbread and biscuits finish the job.
- My South has tar paper shacks but it also has tall glass skyscrapers.
- In my South, people put crabmeat on everything.
- My South has tire swings hanging under live oak trees.
- In my South, grandmothers will put almost anything inside a mold filled with JELL-O.
- In my South, "cobbler" is a dessert, not a shoemaker.
- In my South, the only things that "squeal like a pig" are pigs.
- In my South, ice cream is made on the back porch instead of in a factory.
- In my South, grandmothers always have a homemade cake or pie on the counter.

- My South has bottle trees.
- In my South, we give a firm handshake.
- In my South, "sopping" is an acquired skill and could be an Olympic sport.
- My South is oleander and honeysuckle.
- In my South, we celebrate Easter a month and a half early with a two-week-long party called Mardi Gras.
- In my South, fried chicken is a religion with its own denomination.
- My South has sugar-sand beaches, pine forests, plains, hills, swamps, and mountains.
- In my South, we still open doors and pull out chairs for ladies.
- In my South, we eat hush puppies instead of wearing them on our feet.
- In my South, it's OK to discuss politics and religion at the dinner table. As a matter of fact, it is required.
- In my South, we don't hold Elvis's movies against him.
- My South has shrimp boats and multicolored sunrises.
- In my South, we move slowly because we can.
- My South has covered dish suppers and cutting-edge fine dining restaurants.
- In my South, young boys still catch fireflies in washed-out mayonnaise jars.
- In my South, 50 percent of the dinner conversation deals with someone's genealogy.
- In my South, we don't burn crosses, we worship them.
- In my South, the dogs are still scratching.

Quick Chilling Soups or Stews

Before refrigerating homemade soup or stew, it must be thoroughly cooled.

To speed up this process, fill a large plastic beverage bottle almost to the top with water and freeze.

Cool the soup or stew rapidly by using the frozen bottle to stir it.

Potato Soup

½ lb	Bacon, diced
1 Tbl	Butter
1 cup	Onion, small dice
½ cup	Celery, small dice
½ cup	Carrot, small dice
2 tsp	Garlic, minced
2 tsp	Salt
1 tsp	Black pepper, freshly ground
2 lbs	Potatoes, peeled and cut into ½-inch cubes
1½ quarts	Chicken broth
½ cup	Butter
¾ cup	Flour
3 cups	Heavy whipping cream
1 cup	Sour cream
1 cup	Monterey Jack cheese, shredded
1 tsp	Hot sauce
½ cup	Green onion, chopped

Place bacon and butter in a 6-quart stockpot over medium heat and cook bacon until golden brown. Drain fat and add vegetables, garlic, salt, and pepper. Cook for 4–5 minutes. Add potatoes and chicken broth and bring to a slow simmer. Cook until potatoes become tender, about 15 minutes. In a separate skillet, melt butter and stir in flour to make a roux. Cook until the roux is light

blond and gently whisk roux into soup mixture. Try to be careful not to break up the potatoes. Add remaining ingredients and bring to a simmer once more. Remove from heat and serve.

Yield: 1 gallon

Cooking Tips

Drying Grated Potatoes

Use a salad spinner to quickly dry grated potatoes.

Bouquet Garni

Bouquet garni is a classic French combination of herbs and spices used to flavor dishes.

To make a bouquet garni, put the herbs into a coffee filter and tie it.

Tie the other end of the string to the handle of the pot or pan so you can easily retrieve the bouquet garni.

Vichyssoise

1 Tbl	Bacon grease (or butter)
3 cups	Leeks, cleaned and sliced
½ cup	Onion, diced
1 tsp	Garlic, minced
2 tsp	Salt
5 cups	Potatoes, peeled and diced
1 quart	Chicken broth
1	Bay leaf
1 cup	Heavy cream
½ cup	Sour cream
1	Egg yolk
½ tsp	White pepper

Fresh chopped chives for garnish

Melt bacon grease in a 2-quart sauce pot over medium heat. Add leeks, onion, garlic, and salt. Cook until the vegetables become soft. Add potatoes, chicken broth, and bay leaf. Cover pot and cook on a low simmer until potatoes become tender. Allow mixture to cool for 15 minutes. Combine heavy cream, sour cream, egg yolk, and white pepper. Place the soup base in a blender and purée. Add cream mixture and blend until smooth. Chill completely and garnish with chives before serving.

Yield: 3 quarts

Tomato Soup

18	Roma tomatoes, ripe
1 tsp	Bacon grease (or canola oil)
1½ cups	Onion, minced
½ cup	Carrots, shredded
½ cup	Celery, minced
1 Tbl	Garlic, minced
1 tsp	Salt
1 tsp	Black pepper, freshly ground
¼ tsp	Dried basil
⅛ tsp	Dried thyme
1 quart	Chicken broth
2 cups	V-8 juice
½ cup	Butter
¾ cup	Flour
2 cups	Cream

Preheat oven to 400 degrees.

Place tomatoes on a baking sheet and roast 25 minutes. Remove from oven and allow to cool. When cooled, remove the skin. Roughly chop the tomatoes and set aside, reserving as much juice as possible. In a large heavy-duty stockpot heat bacon grease over medium heat. Add onion, carrot, celery, garlic, salt, pepper, and dried herbs. Cook for 6–7 minutes, until vegetables

Cooking Tips

Salty Soup

If a soup or stew is too salty, add raw potatoes cut into quarters, which will absorb the salt.

become tender. Add chopped tomatoes and their juice, continuing to cook for 10 minutes. Stir often. Add broth and V-8 juice and bring to a slow simmer. Melt butter in a small skillet over medium heat and stir in flour to make a light blond roux. Stir the roux into the simmering mixture and continue cooking for 10 minutes. Add cream and bring back to a simmer. As soon as soup reaches a simmer, remove it from heat and serve.

Yield: 1 gallon

Main Course

Chicken Pot Pie

Chicken Pie

Chicken and Dumplings

Chicken Tetrazzini

Chicken Spaghetti

Fried Chicken

Roasted Chicken

Buttermilk Chicken

Spaghetti with Meatballs

Lasagna with Spinach

Vegetable Lasagna

The World's Last Meat Loaf

Grilled Steaks

Pot Roast

Roasted Turkey and Gravy

Stuffed Eggplant

Stuffed Whole
   Trout or Flounder

Pecan Crusted Redfish

Stuffed Shrimp

Fried Shrimp

Fried Oysters

Cajun Popcorn

Fried Catfish

Hoppin' John

Linda's Macaroni and Cheese

Chicken Pot Pie

½ cup	Butter
½ cup	Flour
½ cup	Carrots, diced
½ cup	Onion, diced
½ cup	Celery, diced
½ cup	Butter beans, cooked
¼ tsp	Thyme, ground
2 tsp	Salt
1½ tsp	Black pepper, freshly ground
2½ cups	Chicken broth, hot
1½ cups	Chicken, cooked and diced
2	**Piecrusts (recipe page 256 or 257)**

Egg Wash

1	Egg
2 tsp	Milk

Preheat oven to 325 degrees.

Heat butter in a large skillet over medium heat. Add flour to make a blond roux. Cook 4–5 minutes. Reduce heat to low. Add vegetables and continue to cook 5–7 minutes. Add thyme, salt, and pepper. Slowly stir in hot

Cooking Tips

Handling Raw Chicken

Rinsing raw chicken in a metal colander is a good way to avoid contaminating counters, faucets, etc.

chicken broth. Simmer 10 minutes, stirring often to prevent sticking.

Add diced chicken and remove from heat. Allow filling to cool in the refrigerator for 30 minutes.

Roll out the piecrusts. Place 1 on the bottom of a 9-inch pie pan. Fill with the chicken mixture. Top with the remaining piecrust and crimp edges to seal. Using a paring knife, cut 6 slits into the crust so the pie can vent. Brush with egg wash.

Bake 1 hour. Allow to rest 15 minutes before cutting and serving.

Yield: 8 servings

Chicken Pie

½ cup	Butter
½ cup plus 1 Tbl	Flour
¼ cup	Onion, minced
1 tsp	Celery salt
1 tsp	Salt
1 tsp	Black pepper, freshly ground
3 cups	Chicken broth, hot
½ cup	Half-and-half
1 Tbl	Worcestershire sauce
1½ cups	Chicken, cooked and diced

Biscuit Topping

1 cup	Self-rising flour
1 tsp	Sugar
½ tsp	Salt
¼ tsp	Baking soda
¼ tsp	Baking powder
¼ cup	Crisco shortening
½ cup	Buttermilk
1 recipe	**Piecrust (recipe page 256 or 257)**

Preheat oven to 325 degrees.

Cooking Tips

Baking Powder

In order to test the potency of baking powder, mix 2 teaspoons into a cup of water.

If it fizzes or foams immediately, it is okay.

If the reaction is at all delayed, buy a fresh can.

Melt butter in a medium skillet over low heat. Add flour to make a roux. Cook 6–7 minutes to make a light, peanut butter–colored roux. Add onion and seasonings. Cook 5 minutes more. Slowly add hot broth and stir until smooth. Simmer 10 minutes. Add half-and-half, Worcestershire, and cooked chicken. Remove from heat and allow the mixture to cool in refrigerator for 30 minutes.

For the biscuit dough: Combine dry ingredients and mix well. Cut in shortening until mixture resembles coarse bread crumbs. Gently fold in buttermilk and mix until a ball forms. Roll out piecrust and place in a 9-inch pie tin. Spoon chicken mixture into pie shell. Drop spoonfuls of biscuit mix over the surface of the pie.

Bake 45 minutes. Let cool 20 minutes before serving.

Yield: 8 servings

Chicken and Dumplings

2 quarts	Water
2 quarts	Chicken broth
1 large	Carrot, peeled and cut into large pieces
1 large	Onion, peeled and cut into large pieces
1 stalk	Celery, cut into large pieces
1	Bay leaf
1 Tbl	Salt
2–3 lb.	Chicken, whole

Place all ingredients in a large stockpot and simmer for 2 hours. Gently remove chicken, cool, and pick the meat from the carcass. Cut into bite-size pieces and set aside. Strain the chicken broth and return to a large sauce pot.

Dumplings

3 cups	Flour, all-purpose
1 Tbl	**Poultry Seasoning (recipe page 254)**
¾ cup	Crisco shortening
¾ cup	Cold milk

Combine flour and seasoning. Use a fork to cut the shortening into the seasoned flour. Add cold milk and mix until a ball forms. Place dough on a floured surface and knead it for 5 minutes. Divide dough into 2 parts. On a generously floured surface, roll dough to ⅛ inch

Cooking Tips

Measuring Cups

To help clean measuring cups which have held a solid fat such as shortening or lard, line the measuring cup with plastic wrap.

thickness. Cut dumplings into 1-inch squares and sprinkle with flour to prevent sticking while you roll out remaining dough. Place dumplings in refrigerator and repeat the process with the other half of the dough.

Reheat chicken broth on high, to a rapid boil. Quickly drop dumplings in broth (make sure they are separated to prevent them from clumping). Once broth returns to a boil, lower heat and simmer for 10 minutes. Add cooked chicken into pot and simmer for 10 more minutes. Remove from heat and allow the mixture to rest for 15 minutes before serving.

Yield: 8–10 servings

Chicken Tetrazzini

1 Tbl	Bacon grease (or canola oil)
1 cup	Onion, small dice
½ cup	Bell pepper, small dice
½ cup	Celery, small dice
2 tsp	Garlic, minced
½ cup	Pimentos, drained, diced and minced
1 tsp	Salt
2 tsp	Garlic, granulated
3 cups	Cooked chicken, diced
4 cups	**Mushroom Béchamel Sauce (recipe page 241)**
½ cup	Sour cream
1 Tbl	Worcestershire sauce
¾ cup	Sharp cheddar cheese, grated
¼ cup	Monterey Jack cheese, grated
4 qts	Chicken broth
1 lb	Spaghetti

Preheat oven to 350 degrees.

In a large skillet, melt bacon grease over medium heat. Sauté onions, peppers, celery, and garlic for 4–5 minutes. Add pimentos, salt, granulated garlic, and cooked chicken. Cook 3–4 more minutes. Remove mixture from heat and transfer to a large mixing bowl. Add the

Cooking Tips

Cutting Onions

To avoid tears when cutting onions, either cut them under cold water or repeatedly wet the knife with cold water.

mushroom béchamel sauce, sour cream, Worcestershire, and cheeses. Mix well. Bring chicken broth to a boil in a large stockpot. Cook the spaghetti in broth for approximately 12 minutes. Drain spaghetti and transfer to the chicken mixture. Mix well and place into a buttered 3-quart baking dish. Cover tightly with foil. Bake 40 minutes. Serve immediately.

Yield: 8–10 servings

Chicken Spaghetti

¼ cup	Olive oil
2 cups	Onion, small dice
2 cups	Carrots, shredded
⅓ cup	Garlic, minced
2 tsp	Dried basil
1 tsp	Dried oregano
2	Bay leaves
2 tsp	Salt
2 tsp	Black pepper, freshly ground
6 oz can	Tomato paste
2	28 oz cans diced tomatoes
1	28 oz can crushed tomatoes
1½ cups	**Chicken Broth (recipe follows)**
1 tsp	Balsamic vinegar
1 recipe	**Pulled Chicken (recipe follows)**
1 lb	Spaghetti
1 cup	Parmesan cheese
2 cups	Mozzarella, grated

Preheat oven to 350 degrees.

In a large heavy-duty sauce pot heat olive oil over medium heat. Add onions, carrots, and garlic. Cook vegetables for 10 minutes, stirring often to prevent sticking. Add basil, oregano, bay leaves, salt, pepper, and tomato paste and cook 5–6 minutes. (This will caramelize the

tomato paste, resulting in a sweeter sauce.) Add diced tomatoes, crushed tomatoes, and chicken broth. Reduce heat to low. Allow sauce to cook for 3½ hours over very low heat, stirring occasionally to make sure sauce is not sticking. Finally, add the vinegar and pulled chicken.

Bring the remaining reserved chicken broth to a boil and cook spaghetti until just tender. Strain spaghetti and add to the tomato sauce. Add Parmesan cheese and stir well. Place mixture in a 3-quart Pyrex dish and top with shredded mozzarella.

Cover baking dish first with plastic wrap, then tightly with foil. Bake 40 minutes. Remove from oven and uncover. Let rest for 15 minutes before serving.

Yield: 8–10 servings

Pulled Chicken and Broth

2 qts	Water
2 qts	Chicken broth
1	Carrot, peeled and cut into large pieces
1	Onion, peeled and cut into large pieces
1 stalk	Celery, peeled and cut into large pieces
1	Bay leaf
1 Tbl	Salt
5 lb	Chicken

Place ingredients in a large stockpot and simmer 2 hours. Remove the chicken and pick the meat. Cut meat into bite-size pieces and set aside.

Strain the chicken broth and return to a large sauce pot.

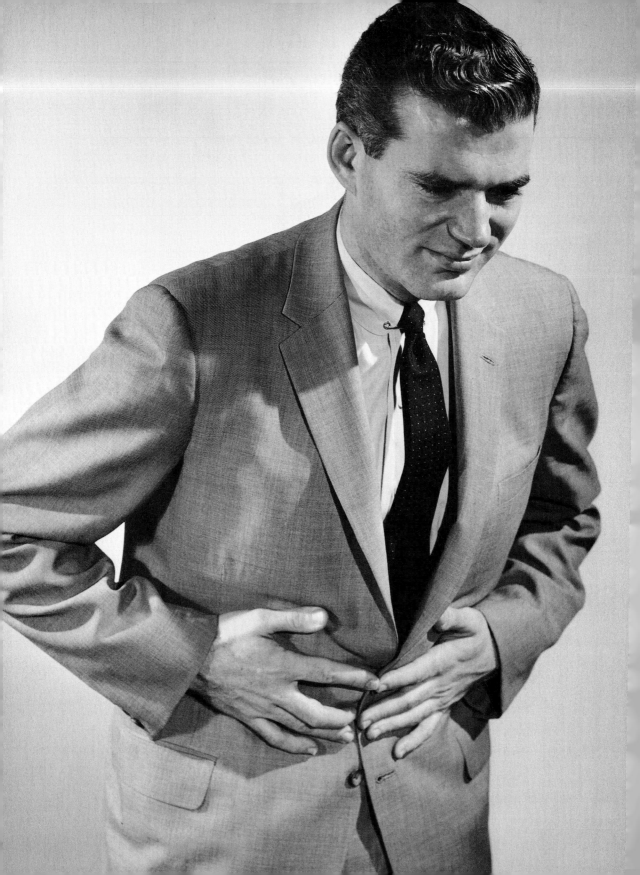

The Great Possum Predicament

I once wrote a column about Hollywood's misconceptions of the South. I had been watching a program in which a stereotypical Southerner, an actor, was eating possum. This actor was excited about eating possum. He couldn't wait to have a second helping of possum. The audience was laughing at him, not with him.

In the column, I stated:

"As long as I have lived in the South I have never eaten a possum. No one I know has eaten a possum. I have never been to anyone's house who served possum. I have never seen possum offered on a restaurant menu and I have never seen possum in the frozen meat section of a grocery store."

That was a true statement . . . at the time. Later, thanks to Alexander Graham Bell, inventor of the telephone, and Al Gore, "inventor of the Internet," I met people who had eaten possum. A lot of people. A whole lot of people. I got to know them intimately. I talked to them at length; I learned their family histories and children's birthdates.

Possum eating is the heated sports rivalry of the culinary world. You are either on one side or the other, and whichever side you are on, you are required to be fanatical about it.

One lady called me a food snob and accused me of being born with a silver spoon in my mouth. My wife laughed at that one. "If only she could see you eating bowlfuls of Cap'n Crunch at 3 A.M." (using a stainless steel spoon, of course).

I asked one varmint connoisseur if possum tastes like chicken. "No," the caller replied, "it just tastes bad." Just as I suspected.

Possums are scavengers. They eat all manner of dead animals. A possum has two choices in life: To be roadkill or to eat roadkill. Thanks to a lengthy, in-depth conversation with another angry caller, I learned that one must catch a possum and put it in a pen for two weeks to flush out its system. "What do you feed them during the flush out?" I asked. "Well, we gave our possums pork chops, collards, corn bread, and butter beans. You know, any scraps from the table." Sadly, no one ever explained the concept of leftovers to this lady. One invitation to a Tupperware party and her family could have been eating day-old pork chops and butter beans instead of pen-fed possum. In a weird, marsupial-munching twist-of-fate, the possum was eating better than its captor.

Another reader told of a teenage prank in which a group of kids fed

a possum a whole box of chocolate EX-LAX and left it in a locked office building over the weekend. I'll spare you the details.

One lady sent a possum recipe from the Drew County, Arkansas, 4-H cookbook. OK, so maybe Hollywood was right about Arkansans' eating habits.

How has all of this possum consumption taken place without my knowledge? I received recipes for fried possum, boiled possum, baked possum, barbecued possum, and possum cooked in a Crock Pot. Readers' comments were all over the place. The most common complaint about possum was that it is very fatty. Another person viewed the excess fat as a benefit. He said, "Possum fat can be used as lard in preparing future dishes." No thank you.

All of this talk of lard and possum was beginning to turn my stomach. One reader stated that "baked coon and sweet potatoes" was better than possum any day. Another sent these cooking instructions: "Skin and gut the possum. Place on a nice pine board and slide that combination into a hot oven. Cook for four hours. When the possum is thoroughly cooked, remove from oven and eat the pine board." Finally, some common sense.

I learned more about the possum than I ever care to remember. Did you know that a possum has seventeen nipples? Well, I know. And now you know, too. Try and get a peaceful night's sleep with that little pearl of information floating around in the back of your brain.

I also heard a possum hunting story from my friend Denton Gibbes, but not a kill-and-eat possum story. It seems he had a "friend" (wink, wink, nudge, nudge) who used to catch possums and put them into burlap sacks. This "friend" would then carry the live possums to town and stuff them into newspaper racks, where the caged and angry varmints would lay in wait for unsuspecting readers of the morning news.

Author's note: A caged possum waiting to scare the bejabers out of a poor unsuspecting reader of the classified ad section lives a more noble existence than the one sitting around in a chicken pen waiting to be flushed and slaughtered.

Fried Chicken

Putting several pieces of celery with leaves into the oil when frying chicken produces beautifully colored and better tasting fried chicken.

Fried Chicken

3 lb	Whole Chicken (fresh)
2 tsp	Salt
1 Tbl	Black pepper
3 cups	Buttermilk
2 cups	Flour

Crisco shortening for deep frying

Wash chicken pieces well in cold water. Place chicken in a bowl with ice water to draw out excess blood. Pat chicken dry and sprinkle liberally with salt and pepper and marinate in buttermilk for 2 hours in the refrigerator.

Season flour with salt and pepper. Heat shortening in a large cast-iron skillet to 365 degrees on a deep-fat thermometer. There should be just enough grease in the skillet to come up just around the edge (halfway) of each piece of chicken. Drain chicken thoroughly and dust with flour, shaking off all excess.

Place chicken, skin side down, in oil and make sure none of the chicken is touching. Cover the skillet and cook for approximately 5–7 minutes, turn, and cover for another 5–7 minutes. Uncover the skillet and continue cooking for 10–15 minutes. Only turn the chicken once. Cook chicken in smaller batches if skillet is too small. Drain

on a wire cake rack with a paper bag or paper towels underneath the rack to catch excess grease (draining straight to a paper bag causes the chicken to sit in the drained grease).

Yield: 8 pieces

Drumstick Tendons

Drumstick tendons turn bonelike during roasting.

To remove these, before roasting, slice through the skin about an inch from the bottom of the drumstick.

Using pliers, grasp the exposed white tendons firmly and pull away from the bone.

Roasted Chicken

1	5 lb chicken, whole
2 Tbl	Light olive oil
1 Tbl	Kosher salt
1 Tbl	Black pepper
1 Tbl	**Poultry Seasoning (recipe page 254)**
½	Onion, small, roughly chopped
½	Carrot, peeled and roughly chopped
1 stalk	Celery, roughly chopped

Preheat oven to 320 degrees.

Thoroughly rinse and drain the chicken. Pat dry with paper towels. Rub the entire surface with olive oil. Season inside cavity and skin with the salt, pepper, and poultry seasoning. Stuff vegetables into the cavity of the chicken. Truss chicken. Place in Pyrex baking dish, breast side up.

Bake 1 hour and 20 minutes. Remove from oven and allow chicken to rest for 20 minutes before carving.

Yield: 4–6 servings

Buttermilk Chicken

1 Tbl	Garlic, minced
1 cup	Buttermilk
1 tsp	Salt
2 tsp	Hot sauce
1 Tbl	Worcestershire sauce
8	Chicken breasts, boneless and skinless
2 Tbl	**Poultry Seasoning (recipe page 254)**
1 tsp	Black pepper
1 cup	Flour
2 Tbl	Bacon grease (or canola oil)
2 cups	**Mushroom Béchamel Sauce (recipe page 241)**
½ cup	Green onion, chopped
½ cup	Sour cream

Preheat oven to 350 degrees.

In a mixing bowl, combine garlic, buttermilk, salt, hot sauce, and Worcestershire. Mix well and pour over the chicken. Allow to marinate for 1–2 hours. After marinating, remove the chicken and reserve the buttermilk marinade. Add poultry seasoning and pepper to the flour. Place bacon grease in a large skillet over medium-high heat. Lightly flour chicken and brown on both sides in skillet.

Poultry Temperature

To judge poultry doneness, insert the thermometer into the leg pit or into the breast as deeply as possible without touching the bone.

Place chicken into a 3-quart Pyrex baking dish. Combine marinade, mushroom béchamel sauce, green onions, and sour cream. Spread mixture evenly over chicken. Bake uncovered 25 minutes.

Yield: 8 servings

Spaghetti with Meatballs

1 batch	**Tomato Sauce 2 (recipe page 245)**
2 Tbl	Olive oil
1½ cups	Onion, minced
2 Tbl	Garlic, minced
1½ tsp	Salt
1 Tbl	Black pepper
1 tsp	Basil, dried
½ tsp	Oregano, dried
¼ tsp	Thyme, ground
1 cup	Red wine
4	Eggs
½ cup	Half-and-half
2 lbs	Ground beef, lean
1 cup	Italian style bread crumbs
1 lb	Spaghetti
2 Tbl	Olive oil

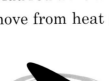

Preheat oven to 375 degrees.

Start the tomato sauce first so that it has been cooking for about 1–2 hours before the meatballs are added. In a large skillet, heat olive oil over medium heat. Sauté onions 5 minutes, add garlic and seasonings, and cook an additional 3 minutes. Add red wine and reduce until skillet is almost dry. Remove from heat and place in a

De-fatting Soups or Stews

In order to de-fat a chunky soup or stew, place a large lettuce leaf on the surface of the liquid in the pot.

The lettuce will absorb the excess fat and can then be removed and discarded.

large mixing bowl. Place bowl in refrigerator 30 minutes or until chilled. Add eggs and half-and-half to the cooked mixture and mix thoroughly. Add the ground beef and bread crumbs. Using your hands, squish the mixture until everything is incorporated. Form 1–2 ounce meatballs and place them on a baking sheet lined with wax paper.

Bake meatballs for 20 minutes. Remove from oven and add them to the sauce. Allow sauce to cook another 1½ hours.

When the sauce is ready, cook the spaghetti following the package instructions. Drain spaghetti and toss with the olive oil. Serve immediately.

Yield: 8 servings

Lasagna with Spinach

1 Tbl	Olive oil
2 Tbl	Garlic, minced
1	10-oz pkg spinach, frozen, then thawed and excess moisture squeezed out
1	10-oz pkg spinach, fresh, cleaned and roughly chopped
½ tsp	Salt
15 oz	Ricotta cheese
1 cup	Romano cheese, shredded
2	Eggs
1½ tsp	Salt
1½ tsp	Black pepper
1 recipe	**Tomato Sauce 1 (see page 244)**
12	Lasagna sheets, cooked until al dente in boiling salted water
2 cups	Mozzarella, shredded

Preheat oven to 325 degrees.

In a large skillet, heat olive oil over medium heat. Sauté garlic for 30 seconds, add fresh and frozen spinach, and cook until wilted. Season with salt. Drain spinach and set aside. In a mixing bowl, combine the ricotta cheese, Romano cheese, eggs, salt, and pepper. Stir well.

Cooking Tips

Boiling Water More Quickly

Speed up the process of boiling large quantities of water by boiling water in two pots, pouring the second pot into the stock pot when both have reached the boiling point.

Ladle 2 cups of tomato sauce into a 3-quart baking dish. Place a layer of 3 lasagna sheets on the sauce and top with ½ the ricotta mixture. Spread ½ the sautéed spinach on the ricotta mixture. Lay down another layer of lasagna sheets and top with 2 cups of sauce. Spread out evenly. Sprinkle the sauce with ½ the mozzarella cheese. Repeat these 2 steps again. Cover the baking dish tightly, first with plastic wrap and then foil. (The plastic will not melt. It will prevent the cheese from sticking to the bottom of the foil.) Bake covered for 1 hour. Remove foil and plastic and bake for an additional 10 minutes. Allow lasagna to set 20 minutes before serving. Spoon the remaining sauce on top of lasagna just before serving.

Yield: 8–12 servings

Vegetable Lasagna

2 Tbl	Olive oil
¾ cup	Eggplant, peeled and diced, sprinkled with 1½ tsp salt
¾ cup	Yellow squash, diced
¾ cup	Zucchini, diced
½ cup	Onion, diced
1 Tbl	Garlic, minced
1	10-oz pkg of spinach, fresh, roughly chopped
2 cups	**Mushroom Béchamel Sauce (recipe page 241)**
1 tsp	Salt
1 tsp	Black pepper
2	Eggs
1	15-oz container of ricotta cheese
1 cup	Romano cheese, shredded
1½ tsp	Salt
1½ tsp	Black pepper
1 recipe	**Tomato Sauce 2 (recipe page 245)**
12	Lasagna sheets, cooked until tender in boiling salted water
2 cups	Mozzarella, shredded
12 slices	Tomato, medium size, fresh

Preheat oven to 325 degrees.

Cooking Tips

Drying Pasta

Hanging homemade pasta over the bars of a wooden indoor adjustable clothes rack is an efficient and space saving way to dry pasta.

In a large skillet, heat olive oil over medium heat. Add eggplant and cook for 2–3 minutes. Add squashes, onions, garlic, and spinach, and cook for 8–10 minutes more, until the vegetables start to become tender. Add mushroom béchamel sauce, salt, and pepper and set aside.

In a mixing bowl, combine eggs, ricotta cheese, Romano cheese, salt, and pepper. Stir well. Ladle 2 cups of tomato sauce into a 3-quart baking dish. Place a layer of 3 lasagna sheets on the sauce and top it with ½ the ricotta mixture. Spread ½ the vegetable mixture onto the ricotta. Lay another layer of pasta and top with 2 cups of sauce, spreading evenly. Sprinkle ½ the mozzarella cheese on top of the sauce. Repeat these 2 steps again. Arrange tomato slices on top of final layer.

Cover baking dish tightly, first with plastic wrap, then foil. Bake 1 hour, remove foil and plastic wrap, and bake for an additional 10 minutes. Allow lasagna to sit for 20 minutes before serving. Use any remaining sauce to top the lasagna with when plating.

Yield: 8–12 servings

The World's Last Meat Loaf

1 Tbl	Bacon grease (or canola oil)
1 cup	Onion, minced
¾ cup	Celery, minced
¾ cup	Bell pepper, minced
1 Tbl	Salt
1 tsp	Garlic, minced
⅛ tsp	Thyme, dried
¼ tsp	Oregano, dried
2 tsp	**Steak Seasoning (recipe page 253)**
1 cup	Milk
3	Eggs
1 Tbl	Worcestershire sauce
½ cup	Ketchup
2 lbs	Ground beef
1 cup	Bread crumbs, coarse

Preheat oven to 325 degrees.

Heat the bacon grease in a large skillet over medium heat. Sauté vegetables with salt, garlic, dried herbs, and steak seasoning until tender. Allow to cool.

Combine milk, eggs, Worcestershire, and ketchup and mix well. Place ground beef, cooled vegetables, and egg mixture into a large mixing bowl. Using your hands,

Meat Grinder

To thoroughly clean out a meat grinder before washing, run through a piece of bread to push out the last of the meat.

squish the meat loaf until you have mixed everything together and all is well incorporated. Fold in the bread crumbs last.

Shape the meat mixture into the form of a loaf on a baking sheet. Using your hand, make an indentation down the center of the loaf (this is where the glaze goes). Bake 50 minutes.

While meat loaf is cooking, make the glaze. Remove from the oven and spoon glaze down the center of the meat loaf and spread over the sides. Return meat loaf to oven, lower heat to 300 degrees, and bake 30 minutes more. Allow meat loaf to rest 15 minutes before serving.

Yield: 8–10 servings

Tomato Glaze

1 tsp	Bacon grease (or canola oil)
1 Tbl	Onion, minced
1 tsp	Garlic, minced
¼ cup	Brown sugar
2 Tbl	Yellow mustard
1 Tbl	Worcestershire sauce
1 cup	Ketchup

Heat bacon grease over low heat. Cook onions and garlic 2–3 minutes. Add brown sugar and stir until dissolved. Stir in remaining ingredients.

Grilled Steaks

6	Ribeye steaks
¼ cup	**Steak Seasoning (recipe page 253)**
3 Tbl	Lemon pepper
1 cup	Dale's Steak Seasoning
1 cup	Stubb's Beef Marinade
	(or other meat marinade: Allegro, etc.)
2 Tbl	Garlic, minced
2 Tbl	Liquid smoke

Heat grill to medium-high heat. Rub steaks liberally with dry seasonings and pat, making sure seasoning adheres to the steak. Set aside.

Mix the remaining ingredients together in a bowl. Place the seasoned steaks in a gallon-sized Ziploc bag (no more than 2 steaks per bag) and pour enough marinade into the bag to cover the steaks halfway when they are lying flat. Squeeze all excess air out the bag and seal. Allow the steaks to marinate in the refrigerator, lying flat, for no longer than 2 hours. Remove steaks from refrigerator 30 minutes before grilling.

Place steaks on the grill and immediately pour a little of the excess marinade on top of the steaks. After the steaks are turned (and you should only turn grilled items once) add a little more of the marinade.

Yield: 6 steaks

Cooking Tips

Meat Thermometer

In order to make sure your meat thermometer is accurate, hold the stem in boiling water for 15 seconds.

If you are at sea level, the thermometer should register 212 degrees.

If it doesn't, twist the small nut beneath the thermometer face with pliers until the temperature is correct.

Secret Second Summer Suppers

I love to eat.

I have always been able to eat a lot. I can sometimes eat an entire meal and then eat another entire meal forty-five minutes later. Of course, these days, I can't eat as much and get away with it. When I was a child, I could do more damage at a dinner table than most.

I have always been open and honest about the various behavioral indiscretions that transpired during my misspent youth. However, some of my most cunning and calculating ruses have remained a secret—that is, until today. I think it is high time to unburden my soul and 'fess up to one of these schemes: my secret second summer suppers.

Let's travel back to 1973, to the story of a twelve-year-old boy who had a passion for food.

When I was growing up, my family ate supper early. Most kids didn't like to eat early. Eating an early supper meant having to leave the playground early. I was glad to have an early supper and sometimes encouraged my mother to have dinner ready as early as four thirty.

Having to go inside while the other kids were still playing was sometimes frustrating, but I had a plan. An hour later, I was able to go back out and visit friends at their house. Friends who, it just so happens, hadn't eaten supper yet. The same kids who gave me a hard time for going in early were now sitting next to me at their dinner table.

My friends' parents were gracious hosts and hostesses. When I showed up, I was always invited to stay for dinner. "Have you had your supper yet, Robert? No? Well, come in and have dinner with us." These unsuspecting parents welcomed me with open arms, having no idea that a twelve-year-old could have such impeccable timing.

Here's how the secret-second-summer-supper scam worked: After eating dinner at my house, I would hop on my orange Schwinn ten-speed and venture out on my second culinary journey. Over the years I learned the eating habits of an entire fourteen-block radius. I knew which mothers cooked from scratch and which mothers were serving TV dinners and fish sticks. I even learned what some friends ate on certain days of the week. One family might have spaghetti every Tuesday; another might eat pot roast every Sunday night. All of them had one thing in common; they were having me for my secret second summer supper.

The only thing that interrupted the secret-second-summer-supper dining schedule was when I rode by a house and a barbecue grill was billowing smoke from the backyard. Jackpot! Slam on the brakes, steak for my second supper! As a child, I could smell an outdoor grill from two blocks away. "Hello, Mrs. Hall, can Stan come out to play?

Oh, I'm sorry, I didn't know you were about to have dinner, I'll come back later. No, I wouldn't want to impose. Are you sure it won't be too much trouble? Why, thank you, I would be honored to have dinner with you. I'm starving, pass the potatoes. What's for dessert?"

I am sure most of the mothers in the neighborhood were gossiping about how the widow St. John never fed her youngest son. "Harold, how could she let her child go hungry like that?"

On the other hand, they might have been saying: "Set another place at the table, Betty. I see the St. John kid on his bike and he's headed this way. Why does he always ride with his nose sticking out like he's sniffing something?" Before long, my olfactory senses became so refined that I could tell whether someone was cooking a rib eye or a T-bone three houses away.

The Roberts family owned a chain of grocery stores. I showed up at their house often. It seemed like they ate steak every night. They also had the best afternoon snacks and breakfast cereals. The secret-second-meal scam worked for breakfast, too, but it seems I was always hungrier after playing all day in the hot Mississippi sun.

I hope I will be able to repay some of these people when their children's children show up at my house around suppertime. First meal or second, it won't matter to me; I'll be glad to feed them.

During summer, the days are longer and the food is better. Now that I have cleansed my soul, be on the lookout. I might just show up at your house around dinnertime. If I do, you'll know what I'm after— my secret second summer supper.

Retaining Heat in Roasted Meat

Allowing meat to rest after cooking but before slicing lets the juices redistribute evenly.

To keep it from cooling too quickly, leave it in the roasting pan, covered, or in a dutch oven with the lid on.

Pot Roast

2½–3 lb	Beef shoulder roast
1 Tbl	Kosher salt
2 tsp	Black pepper
1 Tbl	**Steak Seasoning (recipe page 253)**
¼ cup	Bacon grease (or canola oil)
¼ cup	Olive oil
½ cup	Flour
2 cups	Onion, diced, plus 1 large onion cut into wedges
¼ tsp	Thyme
3 cups	Beef broth, hot
2 tsp	Worcestershire sauce
1 tsp	Salt
1 tsp	Black pepper
3	Carrots, peeled and cut into quarters
2 large	Idaho potatoes, peeled and cut into quarters

Preheat oven to 275 degrees.

Season the beef with kosher salt, pepper, and steak seasoning. In a large heavy-duty skillet, heat the bacon grease over high heat. Brown roast on all sides and place in a roasting pan. Lower heat on the skillet and add olive oil and flour to make a peanut butter–colored roux. Add

diced onions and thyme and continue to cook for 4–5 minutes. Add hot beef broth, Worcestershire sauce, salt, and pepper, and stir until smooth. Pour liquid into roasting pan with the pot roast. Cover with foil and place in oven. Cook 2 hours. Remove foil and add carrots. Return to oven and cook uncovered for another hour. Remove, add potatoes, and cook for 1 more hour.

Yield: 8 servings

Cooking Tips

Freezing Ground Beef

When freezing ground beef, place about 1 pound of fresh ground beef in a zipper-lock bag and flatten it with a rolling pin.

This way, when you are ready to use it, the thinner meat is easier to break off if you don't need the whole thing.

Roasted Turkey and Gravy

⅓ cup	Salt for brine
1	Turkey
1	Onion
1	Carrot
1	Celery stalk
	Kosher salt to taste
	Freshly ground black pepper to taste
2 cups	Chicken broth
¼ cup	Flour
1 Tbl	Kitchen Bouquet

Dissolve ⅓ cup salt in a small amount of hot water; add ice and cold water to equal a gallon of brine.

In an ice chest, place the thawed turkey and enough brine to completely submerge. (This may take more than 1 gallon of brine.) For best results, let turkey sit in brine for 24 hours.

Preheat oven to 300 degrees.

Roughly chop 1 onion, 1 carrot, and 1 stalk of celery and place vegetables in cavity of the turkey. Truss turkey. Sprinkle skin of the turkey with kosher salt and freshly ground pepper (about 1 tablespoon of each for a 14-lb turkey). Place turkey in a roasting pan on a roasting rack. Place 2 cups of chicken broth in the bottom of the roasting pan and place all in the oven. Roast turkey for 12 minutes per pound. Do not baste or open the oven door during cooking process.

When done (turkey has reached 180 degrees on a meat thermometer inserted into the thickest part of the thigh), remove the roasting rack and place turkey on a cookie sheet.

Remove the drippings from the pan. Using a fat separator, remove fat from the juices. Place the turkey fat into a medium skillet (you should have ¼ cup fat; if you do not, add a bit of oil to make up the difference). Heat the broth in a microwave. Add ¼ cup flour to the fat and cook over medium heat for 4–5 minutes, stirring constantly. Stir in the hot broth and simmer until thickened. Add canned chicken broth if gravy is too thick. Add one tablespoon Kitchen Bouquet.

Let turkey rest for 2 minutes per pound before carving.

Yield: one hungry family and a few unwanted relatives

Cooking Tips

Turkey Lifting

To lift a turkey out of a roasting pan: Use two long-handled wooden spoons inserted into either end of a turkey's cavity and keep your hands close to the turkey.

Female eggplants have more seeds and are more likely to be bitter than male eggplants.

1. A female eggplant has a small indentation on the bottom that looks like a belly button. The female has more seeds inside, especially if it is large and mature.

2. The stem spot on a male eggplant is much shallower and in some cases may be flat. It looks more like a scar than a belly button. The male has few if any seeds.

Stuffed Eggplant

4	Eggplants, medium
½ cup	Olive oil, divided
¼ tsp	Salt
¼ tsp	Pepper
2 cups	Onion, diced
1 cup	Celery, diced
1 cup	Bell pepper, diced
1½ cups	Eggplant, diced
1 lb	Shrimp, small, peeled
2 tsp	Old Bay seasoning
2 tsp	**Creole Seasoning (recipe page 252)**
½ cup	Green onion, chopped
¼ cup	Parsley
1 lb	Crab claw meat
1 cup	Cracker crumbs, crushed
2 tsp	Hot sauce
1 cup	White wine

Preheat oven to 350 degrees.

Cut eggplants in half lengthwise. Use a paring knife to cut out the center of each half. Leave about a ½-inch-thick barrier in the eggplants. Reserve removed eggplant for the filling.

Rub the flesh of the hollowed-out eggplants with ½ of the oil. Combine salt and pepper and sprinkle it over the eggplant halves. Place in a large baking dish and bake for 20 minutes.

While the eggplants are baking, prepare the filling. In a large skillet heat the remaining oil over medium heat. Sauté vegetables for 6–7 minutes. Add shrimp and seasonings, continuing to cook for 5 more minutes. Remove from heat and stir in remaining ingredients (except for the white wine).

Divide filling evenly into par-baked eggplants. Pour the wine into the baking dish and cover with foil. Bake for 25 minutes, remove foil, and continue baking for another 10 minutes. Remove from the oven and serve.

Yield: 8 servings

Cooking Tips

Stuffed Peppers

Two ways of keeping stuffed peppers upright during baking are to put them in a tube pan to ensure a snug fit, or in a muffin tin to prevent sliding.

Jill's Sliceable Gravy

I love my wife more than life itself. She is an exceptional person and my best friend. She is an excellent mother. She is smart, she is fun, and she is beautiful. She makes me laugh. She challenges my intellect (so she's got it easy in that department) and she is completely devoted to our family. She is my rock.

And then there is her cooking.

My wife is currently listed among the Who's Who of the Culinarily Challenged. She makes hard-boiled eggs explode. She burns toast. She scrambles eggs until they turn into rubbery green pellets. And any dish she prepares that lists cheese as an ingredient automatically receives twelve times the amount of cheese that was called for in the recipe (she is a practicing cheeseaholic).

But nowhere are her cooking skills more suspect than in the area of gravy.

Folks, I adore my wife, but you can cut her gravy with a knife. As I have always understood the gravy principle, gravy is supposed to be

a flowing liquid that is ladled over a meat or starch. My wife doesn't adhere to that principle. One doesn't serve my wife's gravy in a gravy boat accompanied by a gravy ladle, but rather on a large platter with a serving fork.

Erma Bombeck claimed that her family considered gravy a beverage. Well, in my family, gravy is considered a meat, one to be eaten with a steak knife.

I try to give my wife cooking tips, but she won't have it. I try to sneak over to see what's going on while her gravy is being prepared, but she won't let me near. Judging from the thickness of the end result, you can bet your bottom dollar that whatever is going on in that skillet, there is a lot of flour involved. There is apparently no rhyme or reason to her method. She knows her gravy is ready when it passes the fork test. (To apply my wife's fork test, one must stick a fork into a gravy bowl—or gravy plate in her case. If the fork stands up on its own, the gravy is ready.)

In its simplest form, gravy is nothing more than roux and stock. I run into more people who are baffled by the roux-making process. Roux is nothing more than combining and heating flour and fat (and in my wife's case much more flour than fat). Regulate your heat and stir it constantly.

All that is needed to make gravy is reserved fat, butter, or oil, flour, pan drippings and/or stock, salt, and pepper. My grandmother was fond of Kitchen Bouquet and her gravies always arrived at the table tinted in a rich, silky brown hue.

Wine should never be an ingredient in gravy. Wine is a key component in many sauces, but gravy should receive the majority of its flavor from pan drippings and natural *jus*. The Northeasternbased hip and trendy food magazines always publish Thanksgiving and holiday issues that include turkey gravies with all sorts of foreign items added to them: cranberries, chestnuts, codfish. That is Yankee gravy.

I don't like milk-based gravies, not even the sausage-flecked milk gravy some people pile on top of biscuits. I'll stick with honey and butter on my biscuits. I do like tomato gravy, and perfectly made giblet gravy is food of the gods.

I love the smell of gravy as it is being made. It is a toasted-flour smell. It reminds me of my grandmother's house. When we prepare our daily gumbo in the Purple Parrot Café kitchens, I am taken back to my grandmother's house during Sunday lunch. In her house, when that toasted-flour aroma filled the air, you knew it was time to eat. Gravy was the last dish made before the food was delivered to the table.

Roy Blount Jr. says that gravy is "a personal expression of the soul." If Roy is correct in his assumption, my wife's soul is thick, cloudy, and amazingly pliable. But at least her soul can pass the fork test!

Stuffed Whole Trout or Flounder

¼ cup	Parsley, chopped
1½ tsp	Hot sauce
½ tsp	Salt
2	Eggs and 3 yolks
¾ cup	Mayonnaise
½ cup	Sour cream
¼ cup	Dijon mustard
2 Tbl	Cider vinegar
1½ tsp	Old Bay seasoning
1	10-oz pkg of spinach, frozen, thawed, and dried very well
½ cup	Bread crumbs, coarse
1 Tbl	Dill, dry
1½ lbs	Crab claw meat
10	Saltine crackers, crushed into crumbs
8	Trout or flounder, whole, bones removed
¼ cup	Olive oil

Preheat oven to 375 degrees.

Mix together all ingredients except crab, oil, fish, and cracker crumbs. Gently fold in crabmeat. Fold in crackers until just incorporated. Fill cavity of each fish with stuffing. Rub the entire fish with the olive oil and place on an oiled baking sheet. Bake 16–18 minutes.

Yield: 8 servings

Pecan Crusted Redfish

1 cup	Flour
½ tsp	Salt
¼ tsp	Pepper
½ tsp	**Creole Seasoning (recipe page 252)**
1 stick	Butter
8	6–7 oz Redfish filets

Preheat oven to 325 degrees.

Combine flour with seasonings. Melt butter in a large skillet over medium-high heat. Lightly dust filets in seasoned flour and place in skillet. Lightly brown both sides and then place on a baking sheet. Spread pecan butter over the top surface of each filet. Bake 15 minutes.

Yield: 8 servings.

Pecan Butter

2 sticks	Butter, softened
2 cups	Pecans, chopped
½ cup	Onion, diced
1½ Tbl	Lemon juice
2 tsp	Hot sauce
1 Tbl	Garlic, minced

Freezing Fish

In order to avoid freezer burn when freezing fish, partially fill a Ziploc bag with water and add whole fish or filets.

Then add more water until the fish are covered, and freeze.

Place ingredients in a food processor and purée until well incorporated. Butter may be made in advance and stored in refrigerator. Allow butter to soften before preparing fish.

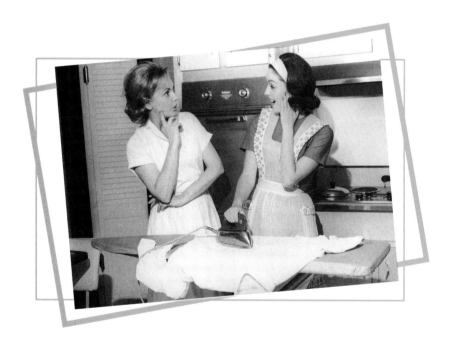

Stuffed Shrimp

¼ cup	Parsley, chopped
1½ tsp	Hot sauce
1½ tsp	Salt
2	Eggs and 3 yolks
¾ cup	Mayonnaise
½ cup	Sour cream
¼ cup	Dijon mustard
2 Tbl	Cider vinegar
1½ tsp	Old Bay seasoning
1	10-oz pkg of spinach, frozen, thawed, and squeezed dry
½ cup	Bread crumbs, coarse
1 Tbl	Dill, dry
1½ lbs	Crabmeat
10	Saltine crackers, crushed into crumbs
¼ cup	Olive oil
32	Shrimp, peeled and butterflied

Preheat oven to 350 degrees.

Mix together all ingredients except crab, cracker crumbs, oil, and shrimp. Add crab and gently fold in. Add crackers, fold in until just incorporated. Oil a 3-quart baking dish. Top each shrimp with 1½ tablespoons of crab mixture. Arrange shrimp in baking dish. Bake 20 minutes. Remove from oven and serve.

Yield: 8 servings

Fried Shrimp

Oil for frying	
2 cups	Buttermilk
1	Egg
2 cups	Corn flour
1 Tbl	Salt
2 Tbl	**Creole Seasoning (recipe page 252)**
2 lbs	Shrimp, large, peeled and deveined

Heat oil to 340 degrees in a large cast-iron skillet. Beat together the buttermilk and egg. Combine corn flour, salt, and Creole seasoning. Dip shrimp into buttermilk mixture and dredge in corn-flour mix. Drop, 1 at a time, into the hot oil and fry until golden, about 6–7 minutes. Remove and drain.

NOTE:

When frying, it is crucial to maintain the oil temperature. Over-loading the oil will cause a severe drop in temperature, causing whatever you are frying to absorb more oil, resulting in a greasy, soggy final product. Keep a thermometer in the oil at all times so that you can monitor the temperature. Also, only bread as much as you can fry at one time. Pre-breading can cause clumps, which will fall off during the frying process. A good method for frying in batches is to preheat your oven to "warm" (200 degrees). Place paper towels or a cooling rack on a baking sheet and place in the oven. Place the already fried objects in the oven, leaving the oven door cracked slightly to prevent steaming.

Fried Oysters

Peanut oil for frying

1⅔ cups	Cornmeal
⅓ cup	Corn flour
2 tsp	Salt
2 Tbl	**Creole Seasoning (recipe page 252)**
2 dozen	Oysters, fresh shucked

Heat oil in cast-iron skillet to 350 degrees. Combine cornmeal, corn flour, salt, and Creole seasoning. Dredge oysters in cornmeal and drop 1 at a time into hot oil. Fry until golden and crispy (about 5 minutes), remove, drain, and serve.

NOTE:

When frying, it is crucial to maintain the oil temperature. Overloading the oil will cause a severe drop in temperature, causing whatever you are frying to absorb more oil, resulting in a greasy, soggy final product. Keep a thermometer in the oil at all times so that you can monitor the temperature. Also, only bread as much as you can fry at one time. Pre-breading can cause clumps, which will fall off during the frying process. A good method for frying in batches is to preheat your oven to "warm" (200 degrees). Place paper towels or a cooling rack on a baking sheet and place in the oven. Place the already fried objects in the oven, leaving the oven door cracked slightly to prevent steaming.

Cajun Popcorn

Peanut oil for frying

1 lb	Crawfish tail meat
⅓ cup	**Creole Seasoning (recipe page 252)**
2 cups	Flour

Comeback Sauce for dipping (recipe page 233)

Pour peanut oil 2 inches deep into a skillet. Bring oil to 365 degrees.

Place crawfish in a bowl, separating the tails. (Do not squeeze the fat out of the crawfish.) Sprinkle 2 tablespoons of Creole seasoning over crawfish. Combine the remaining Creole seasoning with the flour and stir to combine.

Use a slotted spoon to remove crawfish from the bowl. Toss the drained crawfish tail meat in the flour thoroughly. Shake off any excess flour and fry for approximately 2 minutes until golden. Be careful not to overfry the crawfish. Serve with Comeback Sauce (recipe page 233) for dipping.

Fried Catfish

Peanut oil for frying

2 cups	Cornmeal
3 Tbl	Lawry's Seasoning Salt
3 Tbl	Lemon pepper seasoning
8	Catfish, 5 ounce filets

Heat oil in a cast-iron skillet to 350 degrees. Combine cornmeal, Lawry's, and lemon pepper. Dredge catfish strips in cornmeal mixture and shake off excess. Drop 1 at a time into hot oil. Fry until golden (about 6 minutes), remove, drain, and serve.

NOTE:

When frying, it is crucial to maintain the oil temperature. Overloading the oil will cause a severe drop in temperature, causing whatever you are frying to absorb more oil, resulting in a greasy, soggy final product. Keep a thermometer in the oil at all times so that you can monitor the temperature. Also, only bread as much as you can fry at one time. Pre-breading can cause clumps, which will fall off during the frying process. A good method for frying in batches is to preheat your oven to "warm" (200 degrees). Place paper towels or a cooling rack on a baking sheet and place in the oven. Place the already fried objects in the oven, leaving the oven door cracked slightly to prevent steaming.

Cooking Tips

Seasoning Cast Iron

Wash pan in warm, soapy water and towel dry.

Coat the inside and outside with canola oil.

Place skillet in a preheated oven at 350 degrees for 30 minutes, then turn off the oven and let the pan cool inside it.

To maintain a good cast-iron surface: spray skillet with Pam after each use.

Cakewalk

I took my daughter to her school carnival.

I love school carnivals. Along with Christmas parades and high school football games, they are part of what makes living in the small-town South so special.

Upon our arrival, she made a beeline to the ringtoss and the go-fishing booth. There wasn't a crowd at the penny toss so we gave that a shot. The ever popular dunk-the-teacher booth has now evolved into an event where kids throw wet sponges at members of the football team. The success of that event depends on how well the football team is playing. The line was short, so they must have been winning. When you take teachers and members of the school administration out of the equation, the event loses its kid appeal.

I have always been a fan of the cakewalk. My neighborhood was filled with excellent cooks, all of whom had children attending my school—hence, many great cakes to be won (and later eaten) at my neighborhood school carnival.

At a cakewalk, the winner gets to choose any cake he or she likes. What a great event. An Italian Cream Cake is better than a stuffed animal or a handful of hard candy any day. I took my daughter to the

cakewalk at her carnival, but she doesn't eat sweets, so the competition held no appeal. She went to get her face painted while her old man tried to win a cake.

The cakewalk has changed. In my day, it was played like a game of musical chairs. The teachers placed a group of chairs in a circle, all facing out. Then they would play a record (usually a cheesy polka song) and everyone would walk around the circle. While the contestants walked, a teacher removed one chair, leaving one less chair than there were contestants. When the music stopped, everyone scrambled to sit down. The odd man out walked away cakeless and hungry. This process was repeated until there was only one chair and two players. That's when it got serious. Fighting over that last chair was a challenge. I was good at it. When there is food on the line, I am a fierce competitor.

If cakewalking were an Olympic sport, I would have been a gold medalist. I had no problem sending a fourth-grader sailing across the room if there was a caramel cake on the line. I could fight over the last remaining chair with the best of them. Win at all costs, that's what Churchill said.

Nowadays, the cakewalk is played by standing on a number, not sitting in a chair. The numbers are aligned in a circle on the floor. When the music plays, you walk around the circle. When the music stops, you stop and stand on a number. Then the teacher draws a number. BORING! The entire process takes about twenty-five seconds. There is no pushing or shoving. No flying fourth-graders. No sailing chairs. There is no skill involved. It is all based on the luck of the draw.

Note to future carnival goers: It is best to play the cakewalk early in the evening, as all the best cakes are picked first. At my daughter's

carnival, the home-baked cakes went fast. One hour into the event, there was nothing left but Wal–Mart cakes.

I was glad to see that apple bobbing has been eliminated from the carnival process. Bobbing for apples has to be the nastiest event in the history of school-carnival events. Who came up with this? Were a couple of PTA moms sitting around in a planning session one day saying, "I know Thelma Jean, let's have little children stick their faces in a bucket of nasty water that 250 other elementary-school kids have submerged their dirty, sweaty, snotty faces into, all for a five-cent piece of fruit. Surely they'll pay to do that. Never mind that we're in the middle of the cold and flu season." Talk about an event one needs to do early in the evening. If you weren't the first bobber, you got nothing but slobber.

School carnivals make me think of caramel apples, popcorn, pumpkins, the crisp coming of fall, and cakewalks.

Cooking Tips

Puréeing Garlic

To purée garlic, cut 1 inch from the end of a head of roasted garlic and put it tip side down in a potato ricer.

The extruded garlic is nicely puréed, while the peel remains inside the ricer.

Hoppin' John

1 cup	Andouille sausage, small dice
1 cup	Smoked sausage, small dice
1 cup	Onion, diced
½ cup	Celery, diced
½ cup	Bell pepper, diced
1 Tbl	Garlic, minced
1 tsp	Salt
½ tsp	Pepper
1 tsp	**Creole Seasoning (recipe page 252)**
½ cup	Rice
1½ cups	Chicken broth, hot
1 recipe	**Black-eyed peas (recipe page 167)**
1 Tbl	Hot sauce

Preheat oven to 325 degrees.

Place a medium sauce pot on low-medium heat. Place the diced meats in the pot and cook for 6–7 minutes, stirring often to prevent sticking. Add vegetables and garlic and continue to cook 10 minutes. Add in seasonings and rice and cook long enough to allow the rice to get hot. Add the chicken broth and bring to a simmer. Lower heat and cover the sauce pot. Cook 15 minutes (there should still be some broth in the pot). Add the peas and hot sauce to the rice mixture. Mix well and

pour into a 2-quart baking dish. Cover with foil and place in oven for 30–45 minutes. Remove foil and bake for an additional 30–45 minutes. Remove and serve.

Yield: 8–10 servings

Cooking Tips

Keeping a Cookbook Flat

Put a clear glass Pyrex dish on top of open cookbooks to keep them flat, readable, and clean while cooking.

Linda's Macaroni and Cheese

1 tsp	Bacon grease (or canola oil)
1 cup	Onion, minced
2 cups	Half-and-half
1	12-oz can evaporated milk
⅓ cup	Butter
½ cup	Flour
12 oz	Velveeta cut into large chunks
8 oz	Sharp cheddar cheese, shredded
1 tsp	White pepper
2 tsp	Salt
1½ tsp	Worcestershire sauce
1 lb	Elbow macaroni

Preheat oven to 325 degrees.

Heat the bacon grease in a 2-quart sauce pot over low heat. Cook onion 5–6 minutes, then add half-and-half and evaporated milk into sauce pot. Bring to a simmer. In a separate skillet, melt butter and stir in flour to make a roux. Cook until the roux becomes light blond and add to milk mixture. Cook for 6–7 minutes on low, stirring constantly. Remove from heat and fold in Velveeta, cheddar cheese, pepper, salt, and Worcestershire. Stir until cheeses are melted.

While you are preparing the sauce bring 6 quarts of water, and 1 tablespoon salt to a boil. Cook macaroni to just tender. Drain and fold macaroni into cheese mixture. Place in a 2-quart baking dish and bake for 25 minutes.

Yield: 5–8 servings

Vegetables

The Ultimate
   Green Bean Casserole

Spinach Madeleine

Spinach Soufflé

Broccoli Casserole

Squash Casserole

Eggplant Casserole

Asparagus Amandine

Brandied Carrots

Corn Pudding

Creamed Corn

Corn Fritters

Butter Beans

Peas

Turnip Greens
   (Collards or Mustards)

Cookout Baked Beans

Summer Succotash

Delta Tomatoes

Cheesy Tomato Bake

Tea Room Tomatoes

Garlicky New Potatoes

Mashed Potatoes

Scalloped Potatoes

Crawfish Stuffed
   Baked Potatoes

Jill's Sweet Potatoes

Homemade French Fries

Sautéed Mushrooms

Fried Eggplant

Fried Dill Pickles

Fried Okra

The Ultimate Green Bean Casserole

1 qt	Chicken broth
4 cans	Green beans, drained (14.5-oz cans)
¼ cup	Bacon, diced
1 cup	Onion, medium dice
2 tsp	Caraway seeds (optional)
1½ tsp	Salt
1 tsp	Pepper
2 cups	**Mushroom Béchamel Sauce (recipe page 241)**
4 oz can	Sliced water chestnuts, drained (optional)
1 cup	Swiss cheese, shredded
6-oz can	French's French Fried Onions

Preheat oven to 350 degrees.

In a large sauce pot, bring chicken broth to a boil. Place green beans in the broth and simmer 10 minutes. Drain the green beans.

Meanwhile, in a separate skillet, render bacon until it just becomes crisp. Drain excess bacon grease from the skillet and add the diced onions. Cook over medium heat

Cooking Tips

Bacon Grease Disposal

To drain grease from a skillet, grab a wad of paper towels with a pair of tongs, tilt the skillet, and absorb the excess grease with the paper towels.

for 5 minutes. Stir in caraway seeds, salt, pepper, and mushroom béchamel sauce. Remove mixture from heat and fold in green beans, water chestnuts, cheese, and ½ of the canned, fried onions. Place mixture in a 3-quart baking dish and bake 30 minutes. Remove from the oven and sprinkle the remaining fried onions over the top of the casserole and return to the oven for an additional 12–14 minutes. Allow to cool slightly before serving.

Yields: 6–8 servings

Spinach Madeleine

2 pkgs	Spinach, frozen and chopped
4 Tbl	Butter
2 Tbl	Flour
2 Tbl	Onion, chopped
1 Tbl	Jalapeño, fresh, minced
1 can	Evaporated milk
1 tsp	Worcestershire sauce

Vegetable liquor

Red pepper to taste

¾ tsp	Celery salt
¾ tsp	Garlic salt
½ tsp	Salt
½ tsp	Black pepper
8 oz pkg	Cream cheese, cut into pieces

Buttered bread crumbs

Cook spinach according to package directions. Drain and reserve liquor.

Melt butter in saucepan. Add flour, stirring until smooth and blended. Add onion and jalepeño, and cook until soft, but not brown. Combine milk, Worcestershire, and vegetable liquor until you have one cup of liquid. Add liquid slowly to onion/flour mixture, stirring constantly to avoid lumps. Add seasoning and cheese. Stir until melted. Combine with cooked spinach. Place in casserole dish and top with buttered bread crumbs.

Yield: 6 servings

Spinach Soufflé

1 tsp	Olive oil
2 tsp	Garlic, minced
1	10-oz pkg of frozen spinach, thawed, drained well
1 cup	Heavy cream
1½ cups	**Mushroom Béchamel Sauce (recipe on page 241)**
1 tsp	Salt
1 tsp	Black pepper, freshly ground
6	Eggs, beaten
2 cups	Swiss cheese, grated
2 tsp	Hot sauce
⅛ tsp	Nutmeg

Preheat oven to 350 degrees.

In a medium skillet, heat oil over low heat. Cook garlic and spinach 2–3 minutes. Add cream and cook over medium heat until the cream starts to simmer. Place mixture in the blender and purée until smooth. (Tightly fasten blender lid to prevent hot spinach from shooting out of blender.) Combine remaining ingredients in mixing bowl with the spinach purée. Pour into a buttered 2-quart baking dish. Bake 35–40 minutes.

Yield: 8–10 servings

Broccoli Casserole

1 Tbl	Bacon grease (or canola oil)
2 cups	Onion, small diced
1 Tbl	Garlic, minced
1 tsp	Salt
1 tsp	Black pepper, freshly ground
¼ tsp	Dried basil
1 cup	Chicken broth
1 bunch	Broccoli, cut into bite-size pieces
2 cups	**Mushroom Béchamel Sauce (recipe page 241)**
1	Egg
1½ cups	Sharp cheddar cheese, shredded
1 Tbl	Butter
1½ cups	Rice, cooked

Preheat oven to 325 degrees.

In a large skillet heat bacon grease over medium heat. Cook onions, garlic, salt, pepper, and basil for 5 minutes. Add chicken broth and broccoli and cook for 5 minutes more, or just until the broccoli starts to become tender. Remove from heat and mix remaining ingredients together, except the rice. Place ½ of the mixture into a buttered 2-quart baking dish, spread the cooked rice over this layer. Top with remaining broccoli mixture.

Cooking Tips

Storing White Rice

To make white rice last for months, store it in a plastic container with a snug-fitting lid to keep bugs and moisture out.

Bake 40 minutes uncovered. Remove from oven and allow casserole to set 15 minutes before serving.

Yield: 6–8 servings

Squash Casserole

¼ cup	Bacon grease (or canola oil)
8 cups	Squash, cut into 1-inch cubes
1 cup	Onion, small dice
2 tsp	Garlic, minced
¼ cup	Red bell pepper, small dice
1½ tsp	Salt
½ tsp	**Creole Seasoning (recipe page 252)**
2 cups	**Mushroom Béchamel Sauce (recipe page 241)**
1 cup	Sour cream
1	Egg
1 cup	Swiss cheese, grated
½ cup	Parmesan cheese
1 cup	Ritz cracker crumbs (about ½ sleeve)

Preheat oven to 350 degrees.

Heat ½ of the bacon grease in a large skillet over medium heat. Cook squash until very tender (approximately 15 minutes). Stir often so that it does not get too brown. Place cooked squash in a colander. Using a large spoon or spatula, press squash firmly to remove excess liquid.

Place remaining bacon grease in the same skillet and cook onions, garlic, peppers, and seasoning over medium heat for 4–5 minutes. In a mixing bowl, whisk together mushroom béchamel sauce, sour

cream, egg, and Swiss cheese. Fold squash and vegetables into mushroom mixture and place all in a 2-quart baking dish.

Bake uncovered 35 minutes. Combine Parmesan cheese and Ritz cracker crumbs. Spread over top of casserole and bake an additional 10 minutes. Remove from oven and serve.

Yield: 8–10 servings

Eggplant Casserole

2	Eggplants, medium
¼ cup	Bacon grease (or canola oil)
1 cup	Onion, small dice
2 cups	Red bell pepper, small dice
1 cup	Tomatoes, diced, peeled, and seeded
½ cup	Celery, small dice
1 Tbl	Garlic, minced
1 tsp	Dried basil
½ tsp	Dried oregano
2 cups	**Mushroom Béchamel Sauce (recipe page 241)**
2 cups	Cornflake crumbs
¼ cup	Butter, melted

Preheat oven to 350 degrees.

Place eggplants on baking sheet and bake 20 minutes. Rotate and continue baking 20 minutes more. Remove and allow to cool.

Using a paring knife, peel the skin from the eggplants. Cut eggplants into 2-inch cubes.

Place the bacon grease in a large skillet over high heat. When oil is very hot, add eggplant to brown. Add onion,

Dotting Butter on Casseroles

When dotting butter on baked casseroles, shave thin curls off a frozen stick of butter with a vegetable peeler.

This is easier and less messy.

bell pepper, tomatoes, celery, garlic, basil, and oregano. Cook for 5–6 minutes. Stir in mushroom béchamel sauce and pour into a 2-quart baking dish.

Bake uncovered 40 minutes. Combine the cornflake crumbs and melted butter. Spread evenly over top of casserole and bake 10 minutes more. Remove casserole from oven and serve.

Yield: 10–12 servings

Asparagus Amandine

2 lbs	Asparagus, fresh, ends removed
¼ cup	Olive oil
1½ tsp	Salt
1 tsp	Black pepper
¼ cup	Almonds, sliced and blanched

Preheat oven to 350 degrees.

Toss the asparagus with olive oil, salt, and pepper. Place on baking sheet lined with wax paper. Bake 12 minutes. Remove from oven and sprinkle the almonds over the asparagus. Return to the oven for an additional 5 minutes. Remove and serve immediately.

Yield: 8 servings

153

Cooking Tips

Storing Asparagus

To keep asparagus fresh for several days, trim off the ends by an inch and stand them in a small pot.

Add an inch or two of warm water and let sit for 30–45 minutes.

Drain, add cold water, cover loosely with plastic wrap, and refrigerate.

Chitlins

I once wrote a semi-controversial column about eating possum. I was unexpectedly bombarded with phone calls and e-mails from proud and angry possum eaters. I had never eaten possum. I still haven't eaten possum. I began to worry that there were other controversial Southern delicacies that I had been missing out on.

I had never eaten chitlins, either. Chitlins are a very divisive food. You are either a chitlin lover or a chitlin hater. Actually, you are "on the fence" until you eat your first bite, and then you quickly hop onto one side or the other. I wondered about all of the fuss. Being the acutely intuitive investigative food journalist that I am, I decided to delve further.

I hesitated to write about chitlins after the possum incident, for fear that some readers might think my column had moved in a different direction, and that my eating habits had headed down into the deep, dark, endless depths of the culinary root cellar. Some might say I was already in the cellar, and an in-depth treatise on the glory and wonder of the almighty chitlin was an improvement.

The official name for chitlins is "chitterlings," but I don't use that pronunciation. It's silly. It's sort of like spelling "possum" with the formal "opossum." Nobody does it, and I won't start here.

Chitlins are pig intestines. And we all know what runs through intestines. Needless to say, chitlins must be thoroughly cleaned. My friend, Banks Norman, eats chitlins. He has tried to talk me into eating them. Last week, he told me how they were cleaned: He slings them against a tree stump, runs a hose through them, picks off the fat, boils them for four hours, drains and changes the water three times during the boiling process, while skimming and picking more fat. (Banks says the slinging is the best part. He's a pro. He's been slinging the same stuff verbally for years, long before he cleaned his first chitlin!)

Four hours? Slinging intestines against a stump? Having to drain a boiled ingredient three times before you even get to the frying stage? Chitlins must be very tasty to go to all that trouble.

Banks is a kidder. He keeps a few spare kernels of corn in his shirt pocket while eating chitlins. When no one is looking, he will slip the kernels into his mouth and wait for the perfect moment during the meal to spit them out into his hand. "Hey! Who cleaned these chitlins?"

Never having eaten pig intestines, I imagined they would have the consistency of crispy fried calamari with the flavor of smoked bacon—a slight, rubbery texture with a nice hint of piquant pork surrounded by a crispy fried breading of seasoned French bread crumbs. Sounds good to me. I have eaten bacon-wrapped diver scallops, Oysters en Brochette, shrimp wrapped in bacon, and broiled oysters stuffed with a bacon dressing. The seafood/pork pairing is well known. Maybe chitlins and this imagined calamari/pork combination would taste like those familiar dishes.

Andouille sausage is made from chitlins and tripe. I love andouille.

156

One of my favorite catfish houses is Rayner's Seafood House. The Rayners have been frying fish in the same location on US 49 north of Hattiesburg since 1961. Rayner's is home to some of the best fried catfish in Mississippi. They serve fried green tomatoes, fried dill pickles, excellent coleslaw, and some of the best hush puppies you will find.

While eating catfish at Rayner's, I noticed a sign that read:

Chitlins Tuesday Only
Fried or boiled—All you can eat $12.95
Half & Half—All you can eat— $14.95
Dasani Water $1.00

At first I wondered if anyone ever took full advantage of the all-you-can-eat promise. I can't imagine anyone consuming more than one plate of chitlins. I also wondered what bottled water had to do with eating chitlins. Those two foodstuffs seem diametrically opposed. As an uneducated chitlin eater, I wondered if bottled water was required to eat chitlins. I began to worry. Does bottled water make them cleaner? Does bottled water make them taste better? Does it have something to do with the cleaning process that I don't know about? Is there something in chlorinated tap water that interacts with pig intestines and makes you grow hairy ears, a snout, and tusks? Note to self: When eating chitlins, order bottled water.

And why is the combo platter (fried and boiled) two dollars more? I have a theory, but we will get to boiled chitlins later.

I decided to return to Rayner's on the following Tuesday and boldly go where no St. John had gone before—into the culinary root cellar that is the underbelly of the pig, chitlins!

Chitlins Night at Rayner's is busy.

I ordered an all-you-can-eat plate of fried chitlins and a sweet tea. Sensing that I was a virgin chitlin eater, Kim Rayner asked if I wanted them "fried crispy." Sensing Kim was a veteran chitlin server, I replied, "Most definitely YES!" I also ordered a small sampling of boiled chitlins (just to see what they looked like) and an order of fried shrimp (every good businessman has a contingency plan).

In short order, Kim Rayner delivered my plate of chitlins. "How do you eat them?" I asked. "Oh, I don't eat them. But you'll be fine, just use a lot of hot sauce." I should have known right then that something smelled fishy (well, not actually fishy).

Sitting there on the plate, chitlins looked like any number of fried foods. But there was a smell. I can't quite identify the smell, but I can report that I have never smelled anything quite like it. It is a distinct smell, make that a distinct funk.

The funk drifted up from the plate, surrounded my face, and dug into my nostrils, where it kidnapped each individual pore of both sinus passages for the next twelve hours. I went home and changed clothes, still smelled it. I washed my face, still there. I jumped in the shower—lathered, rinsed, and repeated—still there. I had to snort two bottles of Neo-Synephrine to deliver me from this chitlinized trip to nasal hell.

Gathering up all of the epicurean courage I could muster, I took a bite. Actually, I only ate a small piece of one individual chitlin (singular: chitli).

Friends and neighbors, chitlins don't taste anything like calamari. I used hot sauce and ketchup on my chitli and it still didn't taste good. To me, chitlins taste like they smell. Hot sauce doesn't help.

I glanced over to the bowl of boiled chitlins. I don't know what I was

expecting boiled chitlins to look like, maybe Faith Hill's legs or the seat of Jennifer Lopez's jeans. No such luck. Boiled chitlins look like . . . well, like . . . boiled intestines! I resorted to backup plan No. 2 and ate my fried shrimp.

I am sure Mickey Rayner cooks world-class chitlins. The restaurant was crowded, so, as chitlins go, I am sure his are outstanding. I found out from his wife Kim that Mickey is not a chitlin eater, either (every good businessman gives the people what they want).

There were a couple of sweet little ladies seated at a table near me. Each of them had finished off a large plate of chitlins. One lady told me to take the chitlins home and "reheat them for two minutes in the microwave." Thanks, I'll pass.

Then the night began to turn ugly. Other customers began chiming in. One lady said she cooked them in "celery, onions, lemons, salt, pepper, and carrots." "Doesn't that smell bad?" I asked. "I boil them outside, baby." Yes, but doesn't that smell bad outside?

"When it's hot, you don't cook them. Fresh pork makes your blood pressure go up." Frozen pork makes your blood pressure go up, too, lady.

Another nearby customer said, "There are as many ways to cook chitlins as there are cooks that cook chitlins." Yes, sir. There are also as many ways to torture small animals as there are small animals, but you don't see me doing it.

Banks boils chitlins in crab boil. When I complained to him about how my chitli tasted he said, "Mine tastes like crab boil." "Why not just eat crabs or shrimp?" I asked. He looked puzzled for a minute and then said, "I don't know."

I am not a food snob. But if it means I will be labeled a food snob if

159

I never eat chitlins again, then I will proudly wear that moniker like a gastronomic badge of honor.

Before this chitlin research project, I was asking myself how I could have lived in the Piney Woods of South Mississippi for forty-one years and not eaten chitlins. Now I know. Maybe I will let forty-one more years pass and try them again. The year will be 2044 and I will visit the next generation of Rayners, and eat more than one chitli. Then again, maybe I'll just have my usual, catfish and shrimp. An eighty-two-year-old heart can't take that much stress.

Brandied Carrots

5 cups	Carrots, peeled and sliced ¼ inch thick
1 stick	Butter
½ cup	Brandy
1 tsp	Salt
½ tsp	Black pepper

Place carrots on a plate and cover tightly with plastic wrap. Microwave on high for 7 minutes. Remove from microwave and very carefully remove plastic wrap. Melt butter in a large skillet over medium heat. Add cooked carrots and brandy. Cook for 5–6 minutes, stirring often. Add salt and pepper. Remove from heat and serve.

Yield: 8 servings

Corn Pudding

3 cups	Silverqueen corn (4–5 ears)
2 cups	Heavy cream
1 cup	Half-and-half
1½ Tbl	Sugar
2 tsp	Salt
3	Eggs and 3 yolks
1½ tsp	Black pepper, freshly ground
1 tsp	Hot sauce
2 tsp	Onion, minced

Preheat oven to 300 degrees.

Combine all ingredients and mix well. Place in 2-quart baking dish. Place 2-quart dish into a larger dish and place in oven. Pour hot water into the larger dish so water comes up halfway on the sides of the corn pudding dish. Bake 40 minutes. Remove from oven and allow pudding to cool 10–15 minutes before serving.

Yield: 10–12 servings

Cooking Tips

Cutting Corn

Make the task of cutting kernels off corn easier and safer by cutting the ear in half, creating a flat surface.

Place the half ear on the flat side, making it more stable and easier to control a knife down it.

Creamed Corn

8 ears	Silverqueen corn, shucked and scraped to remove milk
2 cups	Water
1 stick	Butter
1½ tsp	Salt
½ tsp	Black pepper, freshly ground
2 tsp	Cornstarch
2 Tbl	Half-and-half

Break 2 of the shucked corncobs in half. Place in a small sauce pot with 2 cups of water. Simmer for 10 minutes to make a corn stock.

Melt butter in a medium skillet over medium heat and add corn and ½ cup of the corn stock, salt, and pepper. Simmer over low heat 10 minutes. Dissolve cornstarch in the half-and-half and stir into the simmering corn mixture. Return to a simmer. Serve hot.

Yield: 6–8 servings

Corn Fritters

1½ cups	Flour
1 tsp	Salt
¼ tsp	Black pepper, freshly ground
½ Tbl	Sugar
½ tsp	Granulated garlic
2 tsp	Baking powder
1¼ cups	Milk
1	Egg
1½ cups	Roasted corn cut from the cob
4 cups	Peanut oil

Combine dry ingredients in mixing bowl. In another bowl, combine milk, egg, and corn. Fold dry ingredients into wet, being careful not to overmix.

In a cast-iron skillet, heat 4 cups of peanut oil to 325 degrees. Drop 1½ tablespoon-sized fritters into oil (cook no more than 8 at one time). Turn fritters in oil so all sides brown evenly. Remove and drain on paper towels. Serve immediately.

Yield: 24–30 fritters

Pot Lids

An easy way to keep track of pot lids is to slide the loop handle of the lid onto the corresponding pot and then hang the pot from the rack.

Butter Beans

3 cups	Butter beans, fresh
4 cups	**Pork Stock (recipe page 242)**
2 tsp	Salt
1 Tbl	Ham hock meat, minced (optional)
2 Tbl	Butter
1 Tbl	Half-and-half

Place the butter beans, stock, salt, and meat in a medium sauce pot over high heat. Bring to a boil. Reduce heat to a low simmer and cover. Simmer 45 minutes on low. Remove lid and stir in butter and half-and-half. Continue cooking until just tender.

Yield: 6–8 servings

Peas

3 cups	Fresh peas, black-eyed, crowder, lady, or pink-eyed purple-hull
4 cups	Pork stock
1 piece	Bacon
2 tsp	Sugar
2 tsp	Salt
1 Tbl	Flour

Place peas, stock, bacon, sugar, and salt in a 2-quart sauce pot over medium heat. Bring to a boil. Reduce heat to a slow simmer and cover. Simmer 30–45 minutes. Remove ¼ cup of pot liquor. Stir flour into pot liquor and pour back into peas. Bring back to a simmer and cook 10 minutes more. Remove from heat and let rest for 10 minutes before serving.

Yield: 6–8 servings

Cooking Tips

Roasting Meats

Roasting meats fat side up will allow for continuous basting.

As the meat roasts, the fat will run down the meat as it renders, adding moisture and flavor.

Slicing Frozen Meat

To make it easier to slice meat very thinly, place it in the freezer for an hour or two.

Partially frozen meat is much easier to slice thinly.

Turnip Greens (Collards or Mustards)

5 cups	Water
2	Ham hocks
2	Large bunches greens, washed thoroughly and torn by hand
2 tsp	Salt
2 Tbl	Butter

Place the water and ham hocks into a large sauce pot and simmer, covered, 1 hour. Add greens to simmering broth and cover. Simmer 35 minutes (collards take longer, approximately 50 minutes). Remove lid, add salt and butter. Simmer for 10 more minutes and serve.

Yield: 8 servings

Cookout Baked Beans

1 lb	Bacon, thick-sliced, diced
1½ cups	Onion, diced
¾ cup	Bell pepper, diced
1 tsp	**BBQ Seasoning (recipe page 255)**
1 cup	Barbecue sauce
2 Tbl	Honey
2 tsp	Yellow mustard
1 Tbl	Liquid Smoke
1 Tbl	Worcestershire sauce
½ cup	Chicken broth
2 large cans	Bush's Country Style Baked Beans, drained

Preheat oven to 325 degrees.

In a large sauce pot, render bacon. Add onion, bell pepper, and BBQ seasoning. Cook 5 minutes. Add remaining ingredients and mix well. Place in a 2½-quart baking dish and cover with foil. Bake 45 minutes.

Yield: 10 servings

Fondue

Fondue hit Bellewood Drive the same year the Beatles broke up.

My mother purchased the first fondue pot on our block. It was avocado green and stood on a metal plate, supported by three stainless-steel legs. There was a space for Sterno under the pot and high above sat an avocado-green top with a small walnut acorn for a handle. The fondue set came with six long color-coded forks to be used for stabbing and dunking foodstuffs and for imaginary sword fights between siblings.

I was nine years old and passionate about food. The fondue cooker was the most astounding thing my brother and I had seen since our mom came home with a pair of pantyhose stuffed in a plastic egg.

The avocado-green fondue pot was displayed in a prominent place next to a wooden bowl that held bananas, an obvious and high-profile location for the cooking instrument that placed our family among the gastronomic avant-garde of the entire subdivision. Visiting friends would ask, "What's that?" I proudly proclaimed, "We fondue, don't you?"

Fondue's development is credited to the Swiss. They combined cheese and wine, heated it, and then dipped bread into the cheese mixture. Years ago, it was a good way to dispense with stale bread. The term *fondue* comes from a French verb *fondre* which means "We'd eat the Eiffel Tower if you dipped it in enough cheese."

Fondue made a big splash as an American dinner-party fad in the '50s and '60s, but people have been fonduing for centuries. There is a recipe for fondue in Homer's *Iliad*: goat cheese, wine, and flour. The addition of alcohol lowers the boiling point so the proteins in the cheese don't curdle. A touch of acid, such as lemon juice or vinegar, usually helps the cheese to melt evenly. Goat cheese was a distant dream in the South Mississippi of the 1970s.

Most fondue recipes call for cheese or chocolate in the cooking pot. Some use flavored stocks or broths. To my recollection, we never ate a traditional fondue meal of melted cheese or chocolate. My mom used Crisco. In the finest of Southern traditions, we deep fried our fondue. And we fried cheap cuts of grocery-store meat, with no marinade, no seasoning, no dry rub—just meat, hot fat, and ketchup—avant-garde cooking South Mississippi style.

"Everyone come over to the St. Johns' house, they're deep-frying meat!" Not since the rollout of Ronco's Veg-O-Matic had the neighborhood seen such culinary fervor.

My older brother asked for a fondue dinner on the occasion of his fourteenth birthday. My mother went all out for this rite of passage and set the table with her finest china, sterling silver, and crystal. She dispensed with the traditional floral centerpiece and placed the avocado-colored fondue pot in the middle of the table, directly under the crystal chandelier.

There we were, in the middle of her formal dining room, stabbing small chunks of discount meat with three-pronged forks and submerging them into two quarts of molten, hot lard gurgling in a cheap metal container supported by three skinny, chrome-plated legs.

Fad dining is dangerous stuff. A sharp, metal instrument submerged in a wobbly vat of scalding hot grease is a fire marshal's nightmare. The birthday dinner ended with a fondue-fork sword fight between my brother and me. Amazingly enough, no one ever called the fire department or the National Safety Council about the St. John boys running through the house wielding red-hot fondue forks like sharp-edged branding irons.

Our fondue pot was mothballed midway through the decade. It was shelved along with the Mr. Microphone, mood rings, puka beads, Ginsu knives, CB radios, platform shoes, dog-eared copies of *Jonathan Livingston Seagull,* and new math. We eventually moved on to more cutting-edge cuisine such as: Quiche Lorraine, Lipton Onion Soup Dip, and Tuna Helper. Years later, the pot was sold at one of my mother's infamous garage sales.

Somewhere out there, in Hattiesburg or in parts unknown, there is another family of deep-fat frying carnivores waiting for fondue to make another comeback so they can make gastronomic waves on their block with our old and wobbly avocado-green cooking machine.

Those were simpler times—times when doors were left unlocked, take-out meals meant eating on the patio, televisions had only three channels, and Michael Jackson actually looked like someone from the planet Earth. Maybe that's what happened to Mike. Maybe he was having a fondue-fork sword fight with Tito and fell face first into the fondue pot. Ah, the price we pay for modern cooking.

Deep in the Piney Woods of South Mississippi, in the small hamlet of Hattiesburg on a quiet street known as Bellewood Drive, the St. John family was—for one brief moment—tiptoeing on the cutting edge of the 1970s cultural and culinary revolution and cooking fondue.

Summer Succotash

3 Tbl	Bacon grease (or canola oil)
2 cups	Squash, medium dice
¼ cup	Onion, small chopped
1	Red bell pepper, medium dice
1 cup	Fresh butter beans, cooked
1 cup	Silverqueen corn kernels, freshly scraped
½ cup	Chicken broth
2 tsp	**Creole Seasoning (recipe page 252)**
1 tsp	Thyme
½ tsp	Rosemary
1 Tbl	Butter

Salt and pepper to taste

Heat bacon grease over medium-high heat. Add squash, onion, and bell pepper. Cook until softened. Add beans and corn. Continue cooking for 2 minutes. Add chicken broth. Reduce heat to low and simmer until almost all liquid has evaporated. Add seasoning, herbs, and butter.

Yield: 6–8 servings

Delta Tomatoes

½ cup	Onion, medium dice
½ cup	Celery, medium dice
½ cup	Bell pepper, medium dice
2 Tbl	Butter
1 Tbl	Olive oil
28-oz can	Tomatoes, diced
¼ cup	Sugar
¼ cup	Brown sugar
2 Tbl	Fresh basil, chopped
2 tsp	Dried basil
2 Tbl	Cornstarch
2 Tbl	Balsamic vinegar
2 tsp	Lawry's Seasoned Salt
½ tsp	Black pepper
1¼ cups	Seasoned bread crumbs
¼ cup	Melted butter

Preheat oven to 350 degrees.

Sauté onion, celery, and bell pepper in butter and olive oil. Cook until onions are soft and translucent. Add tomatoes, both sugars, and both basils. Mix cornstarch in vinegar and add to tomato mixture. Bring to a boil. Add salt and pepper and pour into a greased casserole dish. Mix together bread crumbs and butter. Top tomatoes with bread crumbs and bake 30–45 minutes or until filling is bubbly and bread crumbs are lightly browned.

Yield: 10–12 servings

Cheesy Tomato Bake

2	28-oz cans tomatoes, small dice
2 Tbl	Bacon grease (or canola oil)
1 Tbl	Onion, minced
½ tsp	Black pepper, freshly ground
2 tsp	Salt
1 cup	Brown sugar
1 Tbl	White vinegar
1 cup	Sharp cheddar cheese, shredded

Preheat oven to 300 degrees.

Drain tomatoes in a colander and reserve liquid. Using a spoon, gently press tomatoes to remove as much liquid as possible. In a medium skillet, heat bacon grease over low heat and add onions, pepper, and salt. Cook 6–7 minutes. Add drained tomato juice. Turn up heat, bring tomato broth to a simmer, and reduce liquid by ½. Add brown sugar and cook 5–6 minutes, stirring constantly.

Transfer the sweet tomato broth to a mixing bowl and add the diced tomatoes, vinegar, and cheese. Mix well and place in a 2-quart baking dish. Bake uncovered 2 hours, stirring the mixture after 1 hour. Remove from oven and serve.

Yield: 6–8 servings

Tea Room Tomatoes

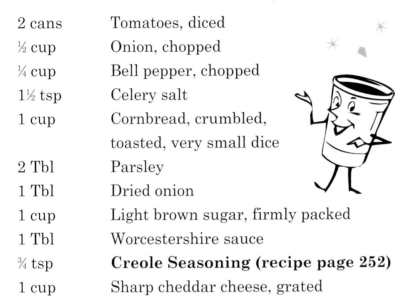

2 cans	Tomatoes, diced
½ cup	Onion, chopped
¼ cup	Bell pepper, chopped
1½ tsp	Celery salt
1 cup	Cornbread, crumbled, toasted, very small dice
2 Tbl	Parsley
1 Tbl	Dried onion
1 cup	Light brown sugar, firmly packed
1 Tbl	Worcestershire sauce
¾ tsp	**Creole Seasoning (recipe page 252)**
1 cup	Sharp cheddar cheese, grated

Preheat oven to 350 degrees.

Combine all ingredients, stirring well. Pour into 13 x 9 baking dish. Bake 30–45 minutes or until bubbly.

Yield: 8 servings

Cooking Tips

Preserving Cheese

Spreading butter over the exposed/cut side of wax-coated cheese will seal and prevent moisture loss.

Garlicky New Potatoes

2½ lbs	New red potatoes, small
3 quarts	Chicken broth
1 stick	Butter
1	6 oz container McCormick Garlic Spread
1 Tbl	Garlic, minced
1 tsp	Salt
1 tsp	Black pepper, freshly ground
⅓ cup	Parsley, chopped

Wash the potatoes thoroughly. Using a paring knife, cut a strip around the outside of each potato. Place potatoes in a large stockpot. Add chicken broth and bring to a boil. Reduce heat and cook at a low simmer for 20–30 minutes, until potatoes are fork tender. Drain potatoes. Place hot potatoes in a large skillet with all the ingredients except the parsley. Simmer over medium heat, stirring gently. Cook 10–12 minutes. Sprinkle with fresh parsley and serve.

NOTE:

New potatoes should be smaller than a golf ball. If you are working with larger potatoes, use a paring knife to cut potatoes into uniform sizes.

Yield: 8 servings

Mashed Potatoes

3 lbs	Idaho potatoes, peeled and cut into quarters
2 Tbl	Salt
1 gallon	Water
½ cup	Butter, cold
8 ounces	Cream cheese, softened
1 cup	Half-and-half, hot
1½ tsp	Salt
1 tsp	Black pepper, freshly ground

In a large sauce pot, add potatoes and salted water. Cook at a low simmer to avoid potatoes breaking apart. When the potatoes are tender, carefully drain. Return potatoes to dry pot and place over heat for 1–2 minutes to remove all moisture.

Place potatoes in a mixing bowl. Using a handheld potato masher, mash the potatoes. Add cold butter as you begin to mash. Next, add cream cheese and mix until melted. Stir in the half-and-half, salt, and pepper. Potatoes may be covered tightly and held in warm place for 1 hour before serving.

Yield: 10 servings

179

Cooking Tips

Drier Mashed Potatoes

After mashing potatoes in a pot, triple fold a paper towel over the top of the pot and return the lid.

The towel will absorb moisture to prevent condensation from dripping back down into the potatoes.

The same will work for fluffier rice.

Scalloped Potatoes

4 large	Idaho potatoes, peeled, sliced into ¼-inch-thick disks
2 cups	Heavy cream
1 cup	Parmesan cheese, grated
2 Tbl	Parsley, fresh chopped
1½ tsp	Salt
1 tsp	Black pepper, freshly ground
1½ cups	Sharp cheddar cheese, grated

Preheat oven to 350 degrees.

Place sliced potatoes in a medium sauce pot and cover with water. Bring to a boil. Turn off the heat and let potatoes sit in water 5 minutes. Drain thoroughly.

Combine cream, parmesan, and parsley. Separately, combine the salt and pepper. Lightly grease a 2-quart Pyrex baking dish. Arrange one layer of potatoes. Sprinkle with ⅓ of the salt and pepper mixture, then ladle ⅓ of the cream mixture over potatoes. Finally, sprinkle with ⅓ of the grated cheddar. Repeat process two more times, but leave cheddar off the final layer.

Bake 35 minutes. Remove and top with the remaining cheddar. Return to the oven for 10 more minutes. Remove and serve.

Yield: 8 servings

Crawfish Stuffed Baked Potatoes

8 large	Baking potatoes, scrubbed clean
2 Tbl	Olive oil
2 Tbl	Kosher salt
8 sheets	Aluminum foil

Preheat oven to 375 degrees.

Oil potatoes, sprinkle with salt, and wrap in foil. Bake 50 minutes. Allow potatoes to cool slightly.

Filling

1 lb	Bacon, thick-sliced and diced
1 Tbl	Garlic, minced
2 tsp	**Creole Seasoning (recipe page 252)**
1 tsp	Old Bay seasoning
1 tsp	Salt
1½ tsp	Black pepper, freshly ground
1 lb	Crawfish tails, cooked and roughly chopped
	Potato pulp from eight baked potatoes
½ cup	Butter
1	Egg, slightly beaten
¾ cup	Sour cream
8 oz	Sharp cheddar cheese, shredded
1 cup	Green onions, sliced

Cooking Tips

Removing Baked Potatoes

Make removing baked potatoes from the oven easier by baking them in a muffin tin.

This way they can all be removed at once.

This can also be done with baked apples and baked stuffed peppers.

Preheat oven to 350 degrees.

Render bacon in a large skillet until crisp; drain ½ of the fat. Stir in garlic, seasonings, and crawfish meat and cook 3 minutes. Remove from the heat and set aside. Cut tops off baked potatoes and, using a spoon, remove as much of the cooked potato pulp as you can. (Leave enough to keep the shells sturdy.)

Using a potato masher, combine cooked potato, butter, egg, and sour cream. Fold in bacon mixture, cheese, and green onions. Overstuff the potatoes and place in a large buttered baking dish. Bake for 40 minutes and serve.

Yield: 8 large potatoes

Jill's Sweet Potatoes

4 cups	Sweet potatoes, cooked, peeled, and mashed
3 cups	Sugar
4	Eggs, beaten
1 cup	Heavy cream
3 sticks	Butter
1 tsp	Cinnamon
1 tsp	Nutmeg
1 cup	Rice Krispies
1 cup	Pecans, chopped
1 cup	Walnuts, chopped
1 cup	Brown sugar

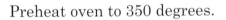

Preheat oven to 350 degrees.

Grease a 13 x 9–inch casserole dish. Combine hot sweet potatoes, sugar, eggs, cream, half of the butter, cinnamon, and nutmeg in a bowl; mix thoroughly. Add sweet potato mixture to greased casserole dish.

Combine Rice Krispies, pecans, walnuts, remaining butter, and brown sugar in a bowl. Mix until crumbly. Sprinkle over sweet potato mixture.

Bake 40–45 minutes or until center is hot.

Yield: 10–12 servings

Cooking Tips

Quick Baked Potatoes

To ensure a shorter bake time for potatoes, wash the potato, coat it with butter or oil, stick a nail in the center, and bake.

This will reduce the cook time by at least 20 minutes, and the butter will keep the skins from cracking while adding flavor.

Jill's Mashed Potatoes

My wife cooks excellent pancakes.

On the 1960s cornball sitcom *Green Acres*, the running joke was that Lisa Douglas, played by Eva Gabor, couldn't cook. All she ever cooked was pancakes; she couldn't prepare anything else. Whenever she tried, it was a complete disaster and an excellent opportunity for comic relief.

My wife doesn't have a Hungarian accent. She is much more beautiful than Eva Gabor and is, without question, more intelligent than the TV character Lisa Douglas. She is one of the brightest people I know. However, my wife reaches the pinnacle of her culinary abilities while cooking pancakes.

My wife is a charter member of the Culinarily Challenged House-wives of America and is the newly elected president of the Hatties-burg chapter. Just last year, she was appointed to the National Board of Regents of the Cooking Impaired and in 2004 she will be the U.S. representative to the worldwide summit for the I.C.C.C. (International Council of the Culinarily Challenged—pronounced: "ick!" It's sort of like the U.N. but no one needs an interpreter and the food is worse).

Regular readers of my column know about my wife's cooking. Her scrambled eggs are hard rubbery pellets, her gravy can be cut with a knife, and any recipe that calls for cheese will receive ten times the amount of cheese called for. At our house, we don't say the blessing before dinner, we pray after we eat. She accepts this. I accept this. We love each other and we get on with life.

This brings me to her mashed potatoes, which usually taste quite good. However, it is not the dish's flavor that I want to talk about. It is the procedure with which she cooks the potatoes.

Normally, my wife won't let me within two hundred yards of the kitchen while she's cooking (it's sort of like a gastronomic restraining order for restaurateurs, but the consequences are more severe and the food is worse). However, I walked into our kitchen last week and witnessed one of the most amazing displays of culinary slapstick since Lisa Douglas hit Eb in the face with a hotcake. My wife was standing at the sink with a paring knife and a steaming hot potato. The potato was cooked but unpeeled. She was juggling the scalding potato with one hand while trying to peel the Scud spud with the other. I was actually impressed with her one-handed potato juggling prowess, but the paring knife was all over the place (judges' score: 9.8 for potato juggling, 4.3 for knife skills, and 1.0 for kitchen safety).

Folks, I never went to culinary school, but I would bet my next paycheck that they almost always teach that swinging a sharp knife while juggling and trying to peel a hot potato is not a safe and sound kitchen practice.

Typically, when one cooks mashed potatoes, they are peeled, then cubed, boiled, and mashed. Not at my house. My wife boils the whole potatoes, unpeeled, and then tries to peel them while they are hot. She claims it is easier this way. If you have never seen anyone do this, you should come to my house on mashed potato night. It is a sight to behold.

Whoever came up with the game hot potato has seen my wife in the kitchen. One would think, after hundreds of years of proven mashed-potato-preparation success, that the time-proven methods of basic mashed potato preparation couldn't be improved upon. Not so at the St. John house. I tried to tell her that centuries of soldiers pulling KP duty have spent millions of hours peeling potatoes, all before they have been boiled. It is a time-proven process. She ignored me.

Being a qualified, experienced yet humble food service professional, I offered to show her how to make mashed potatoes without getting third-degree burns on the palms of her hands. As usual, I was banished from the kitchen. On the way out, I offered to give her some oven mitts to help her hold the scorching potatoes while she attempted to peel them. After that offer was rebuffed, I headed to the bathroom to get the medicated burn cream.

Homemade French Fries

Idaho Potatoes
Ice water
3 Tbl   Salt
1 Tbl   Black pepper, freshly ground
1 Tbl   Garlic salt
Peanut oil for frying

Wash and scrub potatoes. Cut lengthwise into ⅜-inch strips (leaving skin on). Place in a bowl of ice water and let stand 15 minutes. Drain potatoes, rinse, and drain again. Repeat the soaking process one more time.

Mix salt, pepper, and garlic salt as needed. Set aside.

Bring peanut oil to 275 degrees in a cast-iron skillet. Drain potatoes and pat completely dry (make sure potatoes have no water on them or oil will splatter). Cook in 2–3 batches for approximately 5 minutes. Transfer with a slotted spoon to paper towels and place in refrigerator to cool completely.

When ready to serve, bring peanut oil to a temperature of 350 degrees and cook fries 4–5 minutes until golden brown and crispy. Cook in small batches so oil doesn't cool.

Transfer cooked fries to paper towels to drain and sprinkle immediately with a pinch of the salt mixture.

Sautéed Mushrooms

¼ cup	Butter
1 Tbl	Garlic, minced
¼ cup	Shallots, chopped
½ tsp	Salt
½ tsp	Black pepper, freshly ground
2 lbs	Whole, small button mushrooms, or medium-sized cut into quarters
¼ cup	Wine, red or white (dependent on accompanying dish)

Heat butter in a large skillet over medium heat. Add garlic, shallots, salt, and pepper. Cook for 4–5 minutes. Do not brown. Add mushrooms, stirring well. Continue cooking for 8 minutes, stirring often. Add wine and simmer an additional 5 minutes. Serve immediately.

Yield: 8–10 servings

Cooking Tips

Stuffing Mushrooms

For mushrooms that will hold more stuffing, after removing the stem, use the small end of a sharp melon baller to scoop out excess flesh.

This extra flesh can then be chopped up and added to the stuffing mixture.

Fried Eggplant

12	Eggplant rounds
Salt	
Lemon ice water	
1 cup	Flour
2 Tbl	**Creole Seasoning (recipe page 252)**
1	Egg
⅓ cup	Milk
1½ cups	Seasoned bread crumbs
Peanut oil for deep frying	

Peel eggplant and cut into round disks, about the circumference of a mayonnaise jar top and ¼-to ½-inch thick. Marinate eggplant in salted lemon ice water until ready to cook.

Combine flour and Creole seasoning. Combine egg and milk.

To fry eggplant rounds, lightly dust in seasoned flour, shake off excess, dip in the egg wash, and coat with bread crumbs. Fry a few at a time at 350 degrees until medium brown and crispy. Do not overload the oil. Drain on paper towels.

Yield: 12 servings

NOTE:

When frying, it is crucial to maintain the oil temperature. Overloading the oil will cause a severe drop in temperature, causing whatever you are frying to absorb more oil, resulting in a greasy, soggy final product.

Keep a thermometer in the oil at all times so that you can monitor the temperature. Also, only bread as much as you can fry at one time. Pre-breading can cause clumps, which will fall off during the frying process. A good method for frying in batches is to preheat your oven to "warm" (200 degrees). Place paper towels or a cooling rack on a baking sheet and place in the oven. Place the already fried objects in the oven, leaving the oven door cracked slightly to prevent steaming.

Protecting Nonstick Pans

To protect the finish on stacked, nonstick pans, place double sheets of folded paper towels between them.

Fried Dill Pickles

Peanut oil for frying

2 cups	Milk
2	Eggs, beaten
2 cups	Cornmeal
3 Tbl	**Creole Seasoning (recipe page 252)**
1 jar	Dill pickle slices, preferably crinkle cut

Heat oil in a cast-iron skillet to 360 degrees on a deep fat thermometer.

Combine milk and eggs. Combine cornmeal and seasoning. Drain pickles thoroughly. Working in small batches, dip pickles in egg wash to coat all slices. Transfer pickles to cornmeal. Gently toss pickles in cornmeal until fully covered.

Fry in small batches until crispy (approximately 4 minutes). If you fry too many at once, the breading will not stick. Drain on paper towels. Fried dill pickles will not hold, so eat them as soon as possible.

Yield: 8–10 servings

Fried Okra

Peanut oil for frying

1 cup	Flour, all-purpose
1 Tbl	**Creole Seasoning (recipe page 252)**
1 tsp	Salt
2 cups	Buttermilk
1	Egg
1½ cups	Cornmeal
½ cup	Corn flour
1 Tbl	Salt
3 cups	Okra, fresh sliced

Heat oil in a cast-iron skillet to 325 degrees. Mix the flour, Creole seasoning, and salt in a bowl. Beat together the buttermilk and egg in a second bowl. In a third bowl, combine cornmeal, corn flour, and salt.

Place the okra in the seasoned flour first, knock off excess flour, and place in buttermilk mixture. Drain well. Coat with cornmeal mixture and drop into fryer. Fry until golden, approximately 7 minutes.

NOTE:

When frying, it is crucial to maintain the oil temperature. Over-loading the oil will cause a severe drop in temperature, causing whatever you are frying to absorb more oil, resulting in a greasy, soggy final product. Keep a thermometer in the oil at all times so that

you can monitor the temperature. Also, only bread as much as you can fry at one time. Pre-breading can cause clumps, which will fall off during the frying process. A good method for frying in batches is to preheat your oven to "warm" (200 degrees). Place paper towels or a cooling rack on a baking sheet and place in the oven. Place the already fried objects in the oven, leaving the oven door cracked slightly to prevent steaming.

Breads

Sunday Dinner Biscuits

2 cups	Flour, self-rising
⅓ cup	Shortening, butter, or lard
⅔–¾ cup	Milk or buttermilk

Preheat oven to 500 degrees.

Combine flour and shortening in mixing bowl. Work shortening pieces into flour with a pastry cutter until they are the size of small peas. Gradually stir in milk or buttermilk. Add only enough to moisten the flour and hold the dough together.

Transfer dough to a lightly floured surface. Knead gently 2–3 strokes. Using a light touch, pat or roll the dough to a ¼-inch thickness. Cut with a floured 2-inch biscuit cutter, leaving as little dough between cuts as possible. Gather remaining dough and re-roll one time. Discard scraps after second cutting.

Place biscuits on a baking sheet with sides touching for soft, Southern-style biscuits. If you prefer biscuits with crisp sides, place biscuits close together but not touching.

Bake 8–10 minutes, or until golden brown. Serve hot out of the oven.

Yield: 12 biscuits

Cooking Tips

Proofing Bread

The microwave is a perfect place for proofing bread.

Simply heat a measuring cup of water to the boiling point, turn off the microwave, and place the dough inside.

The preheated water keeps the dough at a warm temperature while it proofs in a moist, draft free environment, regardless of the ambient humidity.

Cooking
Tips

Cutting Butter
into Flour

When you don't want to use the food processor to cut butter, use the cheese grater to grate frozen sticks of butter into the dry ingredients.

Light Buttermilk Biscuits

2 cups	Flour, self-rising
2 tsp	Sugar
¼ tsp	Salt
¼ tsp	Baking soda
½ cup	Crisco shortening
¾ cup	Buttermilk
¼ cup	Butter, melted, for brushing the tops

Preheat oven to 375 degrees.

Combine all dry ingredients. Add shortening and use a pastry cutter or fork to blend in the shortening. The mixture should look like coarse meal. Knead in the buttermilk; the mixture will be slightly sticky. (Adding more flour will result in a denser biscuit.)

Place dough on a lightly floured surface. Using a floured rolling pin, roll dough to ½-inch thickness. Cut biscuits and place on baking sheet. Brush tops with butter.

Bake for 14–16 minutes, or until golden brown.

Yield: 12–14 biscuits

Yeast Biscuits

Butter, melted

1 pkg	Active, dry yeast
2 Tbl	Water, warm (105–115 degrees)
5 cups	Flour, self-rising
¼ cup	Sugar
½ tsp	Baking soda
1 cup	Crisco shortening
2 cups	Buttermilk

Preheat oven to 400 degrees.

Grease baking pan with melted butter. Dissolve yeast in warm water. Set aside. In mixing bowl, combine flour, sugar, and baking soda. With pastry cutter or fork, cut in shortening until mixture resembles coarse meal. Combine buttermilk and yeast water.

Gradually add liquids to flour mixture, stirring with fork until flour is moistened. Turn dough onto lightly floured surface and roll out ½ inch thick. Cut with 2-inch biscuit cutter, dipping cutter into flour between cuts. Press cutter straight down without twisting for straight-sided, evenly shaped biscuits. Place close together in prepared pan. Cover with damp cloth and let rise 1 hour (dough will not double in size).

Bake for 15–20 minutes or until brown. Brush tops with melted butter while hot.

Yield: 30–40 biscuits

Icebox Roll Dough

1 cup	Boiling water
1 cup	Shortening or 2 sticks of butter
1 cup	Sugar
1½ tsp	Salt
2	Eggs, large
2 pkgs	Yeast
1 cup	Warm water
Dash	Sugar
6 cups	Flour

Pour water over shortening, sugar, and salt. Blend and let cool. Add eggs and beat well. Let yeast stand in water with a dash of sugar until bubbly.

Add yeast mixture to shortening mixture when it is absolutely cool. Then beat in flour. Cover and refrigerate 3–4 hours.

Remove dough from refrigerator and knead with any extra flour you may need. Roll out, form, or cut as needed. Let rolls rise until doubled and bake at 350 degrees until done and nicely browned.

Dough can be held in refrigerator before the kneading/proofing stage for 5 days (dough must be wrapped tightly with plastic wrap to keep air from reaching it). To bake, pull out the desired amount, knead, proof, and bake.

Yield: A lot

Basic Corn Bread

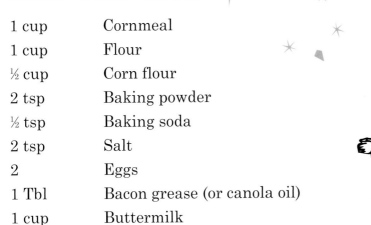

1 cup	Cornmeal
1 cup	Flour
½ cup	Corn flour
2 tsp	Baking powder
½ tsp	Baking soda
2 tsp	Salt
2	Eggs
1 Tbl	Bacon grease (or canola oil)
1 cup	Buttermilk
1 cup	Milk

Preheat oven to 350 degrees.

In a mixing bowl, combine all dry ingredients and mix well. In a separate bowl, whisk wet ingredients. Fold the wet ingredients into the dry ingredients. Do not overmix. Pour batter into a greased cast-iron skillet or a buttered 2-quart baking dish and bake for 20–25 minutes.

Yield: 8 servings

Yankee Corn Bread

1 cup	Flour, all-purpose, unbleached
1 cup	Cornmeal, self-rising
6 Tbl	Sugar
1 tsp	Baking powder
½ tsp	Salt
1 cup	Half-and-half
⅓ cup	Butter, melted (or oil)
1	Egg, large and slightly beaten

Preheat oven to 400 degrees.

Grease an 8 x 8 inch baking pan or cast-iron skillet with vegetable shortening, bacon grease, or nonstick cooking spray. Sift flour, cornmeal, sugar, baking powder and salt into a mixing bowl. Form a well in the mixture and add half-and-half, butter, and egg. Stir until just combined. Do not overwork batter. Bake to golden brown or until a toothpick inserted in the center comes out clean (approximately 12–15 minutes, depending on oven).

Yield: 6–8 pieces

Jalapeño Corn Bread Muffins

⅓ cup	Butter
1 Tbl	Fresh jalapeños, minced
1½ cups	Fresh cut corn and corn pulp
1½ cups	Flour
1¼ cups	Cornmeal
½ tsp	Baking soda
1 tsp	Baking powder
2 tsp	Salt
½ tsp	Black pepper, freshly ground
1 cup	Sharp cheddar cheese, shredded
2	Eggs
1 tsp	Hot sauce
Nonstick cooking spray	

Preheat oven to 375 degrees.

Place butter, jalapeños, and corn in a small skillet and cook over low heat for three to four minutes. Let cool.

In a mixing bowl, combine flour, cornmeal, baking soda, baking powder, salt, pepper, and cheddar cheese and mix well.

In another mixing bowl, combine corn mixture, eggs, and hot sauce and mix well. Add dry ingredients to wet ingredients and fold the mixture until just combined. Do not overwork the batter.

Spray muffin tins with nonstick spray and fill ⅔ full with batter. Bake 14–17 minutes to golden brown.

Yield: 18–24 muffins

Creamed Corn Corn Bread

Nonstick cooking spray

1 cup	Flour, all-purpose, unbleached
1 cup	Cornmeal
2 tsp	Baking powder
1 Tbl	Salt
1 cup	**Creamed Corn (recipe page 164)**
1	Egg, large
¾ cup	Milk
2 Tbl	Honey
2 Tbl	Butter, unsalted and melted

Preheat oven to 425 degrees.

Grease an 8 x 8 or 9 x 9 inch baking pan with nonstick cooking spray. Sift flour, cornmeal, baking powder, and salt into a large bowl. Stir mixture briefly.

Separately, whisk together creamed corn, egg, milk, honey, and butter until honey is dissolved. Add wet ingredients to dry ingredients and stir until just combined. Do not overwork batter.

Pour batter into pan and bake 20–26 minutes, or until golden.

Yield: 9–12 pieces

Hush Puppies

1½ cups	Cornmeal
¾ cup	Flour
2 tsp	Baking powder
½ tsp	Baking soda
1 Tbl	Sugar
1 tsp	Lawry's Seasoned Salt
1 tsp	**Creole Seasoning (recipe page 252)**
¼ cup	Yellow onion, minced
¼ cup	Green onion, minced
1 cup	Buttermilk
2 Tbl	Bacon grease, melted (or canola oil)
1 tsp	Hot sauce
2	Eggs, beaten well

Peanut oil for frying

In one bowl, combine cornmeal, flour, baking powder, baking soda, sugar, Lawry's, and Creole Seasoning. In another, combine remaining ingredients. Gently fold the wet ingredients into the dry and mix until everything is combined. Do not overwork batter.

Heat oil to 325 degrees in a cast-iron skillet. Shape batter into small round balls and drop into oil. Fry until brown, 7–8 minutes. Remove, drain, and serve.

Yield: approximately 30 hush puppies

Desserts and Sweets

Joan Holland's Almost
Heaven Banana Pudding

Bridal Pudding

Caramel Custard

Chocolate Pie

Lemon Pie

Italian Cream Cake

Pound Cake

Strawberry Shortcake

Pecan Brownies

Oatmeal Raisin Cookies

Shortbread Cookies

Sugar Cookies

Pralines

Pineapple Sherbet

Joan Holland's
Almost Heaven Banana Pudding

1 cup	Sugar
6 Tbl	Flour
	Pinch of salt
4	Egg yolks (reserve whites for meringue)
2 cups	Milk
2 tsp	Vanilla
6 Tbl	Butter
Vanilla wafers	
4	Bananas, ripe, peeled and sliced

Preheat oven to 350 degrees.

Combine sugar, flour, salt, eggs, milk, and vanilla in a small nonreactive sauce pot. Cook over low heat, stirring constantly until the custard thickens. Remove from heat, stir in butter until dissolved.

Butter a 2-quart baking dish. Arrange the vanilla wafers around the outside and across the bottom of the baking dish. Spread a layer of custard over the wafers. Place sliced bananas on top of custard and spoon the remaining custard over bananas, spreading evenly.

Preserving Overripe Bananas

To preserve overripe bananas for banana bread, simply put them in a plastic freezer bag, seal, and freeze.

When ready to use, thaw until softened.

Meringue

4	Egg whites
6 Tbl	Sugar
½ tsp	Cream of tartar

Beat the egg whites with an electric mixer. When they start to increase in volume, add the sugar and cream of tartar. Continue to beat until soft peaks form. Spread over the pudding and bake at 350 degrees until golden, about 8–10 minutes. Allow pudding to cool completely before serving (refrigerate at least 4 hours).

Yield: 8–10 servings

Bridal Pudding

2 envelopes	Gelatin
½ cup	Cold water
⅓ cup	Boiling water
6	Egg whites
¼ tsp	Salt
¾ cup	Sugar
1½ cups	Heavy cream
1 tsp	Vanilla
1 pat	Butter
1 cup	Flaked coconut

Soften gelatin in cold water. Pour in boiling water and stir to dissolve.

Beat egg whites stiff, add salt, and gradually beat in sugar. Fold gelatin into whites.

In a separate mixing bowl, whip cream stiff and add vanilla. Fold cream into whites (don't stir). Rub bottom and sides of springform pan (or glass bowl) with butter. Sprinkle bottom of bowl with ½ cup coconut and pour in cream mixture. Top with remaining coconut and chill 4 hours or overnight. Unmold and serve with Custard Sauce **(recipe page 212)** and sweetened strawberries.

(recipe page 212)

Cooking Tips

Cutting Cheesecake

To make cheesecake cutting easier, use dental floss held tightly between two fingers.

Press it firmly through the diameter of cake and into the crust letting go of one end and pulling it through the cake at the bottom.

Whipped Eggs

For best results, allow eggs to come to room temperature before beating.

Adding a little water instead of milk will create more volume and a fluffier product.

Custard Sauce

3 cups	Milk
6	Egg yolks, beaten until lemon-colored
½ cup	Sugar, add gradually along with
⅛ tsp	Salt
1 tsp	Vanilla extract
1 tsp	Almond extract

Scald milk. Pour scalded milk into a double boiler. Add eggs, sugar, and salt, stirring constantly (do not boil), until thickened. Strain and cool. Add vanilla and almond. Chill thoroughly. Beat sauce with egg beater.

Caramel Custard

1 cup	Sugar
⅓ cup	Water
3½ cups	Milk
¾ cup	Sugar
6	Eggs
1½ Tbl	Vanilla extract
⅛ tsp	Salt

Preheat oven to 325 degrees.

Arrange 8 oven-proof bouillon cups in a baking dish; the sides of the baking dish should be as tall as the bouillon cups. Place sugar and water in a skillet with a flat, heavy bottom. Place over medium heat and cook until sugar caramelizes. Pour liquid caramel into bouillon cups.

Meanwhile, heat milk and half of the sugar in a small sauce pot just until it begins to boil. Combine eggs, remaining sugar, vanilla, and salt and whisk together. Slowly pour hot milk into the egg mixture while stirring constantly. Divide the mixture into the bouillon cups. Pour boiling hot water into the baking dish and cover the cups with a sheet of parchment paper. Bake 40 minutes.

Chill completely. Use a paring knife to go around the custards and unmold onto serving dishes.

Yield: 8 servings

Storing Chocolate

Chocolate will last indefinitely when stored in an airtight container in a cooler.

At room temperature, white and milk chocolate should be used within 5 months, and dark chocolate should be used within 18–20 months.

Chocolate Pie

1 cup plus 2 Tbl	Sugar
¾ cup	Heavy cream
¾ cup	Buttermilk
3½ Tbl	Cornstarch
Pinch	Salt
4	Egg yolks, reserve whites for meringue
3 ounces	Semisweet chocolate, high quality
1 Tbl	Butter
¾ tsp	Vanilla
1 (9 inch)	**Pie Crust, baked (recipe page 256 or 257)**

In a small saucepan combine the sugar, heavy cream, buttermilk, cornstarch, and salt and whisk until smooth. Place over medium-high heat, and bring to a boil, whisking from time to time, allowing the sugar and cornstarch to dissolve and the mixture to thicken (about 5 minutes). Continue cooking at a low boil for an additional 5 minutes, whisking constantly.

In a mixing bowl, beat egg yolks lightly. Pour ½ cup of the hot mixture into the egg yolks and whisk thoroughly. Pour the egg yolk mixture into the saucepan and whisk over the heat until thoroughly combined (about 30 seconds).

Pour mixture into a mixing bowl, and whisk in the chocolate, butter, and vanilla. Continue whisking until thoroughly combined (mixture will be very thick). Pour the chocolate batter into the prepared Pie Crust and set aside.

Meringue

4	Egg whites
6 Tbl	Sugar
½ tsp	Cream of tartar

Beat the egg whites with an electric mixer. When they start to increase in volume, add the sugar and cream of tartar. Continue to beat until soft peaks form. Spread over the pie and bake at 350 degrees until golden, about 8–10 minutes. Allow pie to cool completely before serving (refrigerate at least 4 hours).

Yield: 8 servings

Moistening Pie Dough

When making pie crust, rather than trying to sprinkle water evenly over flour mixture one tablespoon at a time, simply put the recommended amount of water into a small spray bottle and spray as needed onto the flour mixture.

This allows for a more even distribution.

Lemon Pie

6 Tbl	Cornstarch
1½ cups	Sugar
3	Lemons, zest and juice
4	Egg yolks
	(reserve the whites for the meringue)
2 cups	Water, boiling
1	**Pie crust, pre-baked (recipe page 256 or 257)**

Combine the first 4 ingredients and beat together. Continue to stir and add the boiling water. Place mixture in a nonreactive sauce pot and cook over low-medium heat until mixture thickens. Pour into the baked pie shell and set aside.

Meringue

4	Egg whites
6 Tbl	Sugar
½ tsp	Cream of tartar

Beat the egg whites with an electric mixer. When they start to increase in volume, add the sugar and cream of tartar. Continue to beat until soft peaks form. Spread over the pie and bake at 350 degrees until golden, about 8–10 minutes. Allow pie to cool completely before serving.

Yield: 8 servings

Italian Cream Cake

1 cup	Butter, softened
2 cups	Sugar
5 large	Eggs, separated
2½ cups	Flour, all-purpose
1 tsp	Baking soda
1 cup	Buttermilk
⅔ cup	Pecans, finely chopped
1 tsp	Vanilla extract
1 can	Flaked coconut (3½ oz)
½ tsp	Cream of tartar
3 Tbl	Grand Marnier
1 recipe	**Cream Cheese Frosting (recipe page 218)**

Grease and flour three 9-inch round cake pans. Line pans with wax paper; grease paper and set aside.

Beat butter with an electric mixer at medium speed until creamy; gradually add sugar, beating well. Add egg yolks, one at a time, beating after each addition. Combine flour and baking soda. Add buttermilk and flour mixture alternately, beginning and ending with flour mixture. Stir in pecans, vanilla, and coconut.

Beat egg whites at high speed in a large bowl until

Silky Cake

To give your cakes a molten, silky look, frost the sides and top and smooth as usual.

Then use a hair dryer to slightly melt the frosting for a smooth, lustrous appearance.

foamy. Add cream of tartar; beat until stiff peaks form. Gently fold beaten egg whites into batter. Pour batter into prepared pans.

Bake at 350 degrees for 25–30 minutes or until a wooden pick inserted in center comes out clean. Let cool in pans 10 minutes, remove from pans; peel off wax paper and let cool completely on wire racks. Brush each cake layer with 1 tablespoon Grand Marnier. Let stand 10 minutes. Spread cream cheese frosting between layers and on sides and top of cake.

Cream Cheese Frosting

1 (8 oz) pkg	Cream cheese, softened
1 (3 oz) pkg	Cream cheese, softened
¾ cup	Butter, softened
1½ cups	Powdered sugar, sifted
1½ cups	Pecans, chopped
1 Tbl	Vanilla extract

Beat first 3 ingredients with an electric mixer at medium speed until smooth. Gradually add powdered sugar, beating until light and fluffy; stir in pecans and vanilla.

Yield: Not enough

Pound Cake

1 lb	Butter
1 lb	Sugar
6	Eggs
2 tsp	Vanilla
3 cups	Cake flour
½ tsp	Salt
½ cup	Buttermilk

Preheat oven to 325 degrees.

Using an electric mixer with a paddle attachment, cream the butter and sugar until light and fluffy. Beat in eggs, 1 at a time. Add vanilla. Sift together the flour and salt and add to butter mixture. With the mixer running, slowly add buttermilk. Beat 4–5 minutes, until the batter is very smooth. Pour into a large buttered and floured loaf pan. Place in the center of the oven and bake for 1 hour and 20 minutes. Be very careful not to slam the oven door or disturb the cake in any way while baking, or it will fall. A toothpick should come out clean when done.

Yield: 1 large loaf

Cooking Tips

Tube Pans

Covering the hole of a tube pan with an inverted paper cup will make filling the pan with batter easier and less messy.

Protecting Pastry Edge from Burning

To protect the edge of a tart shell from burning before the bottom can cook through:

1. Invert the ring of a second, larger tart pan over the crust and continue baking.

2. Cut the center out of a disposable foil pie plate and place the trimmed pie plate, top side down, over the rim of the crust during baking.

Strawberry Shortcake
Cakes

2 cups	Flour, self-rising
¼ cup	Sugar
⅛ tsp	Salt
½ cup	Crisco shortening
¾ cup	Buttermilk
3 Tbl	Milk
3 Tbl	Sugar

Preheat oven to 375 degrees.

Combine all dry ingredients. Add shortening and use a pastry cutter or fork to blend it in. The mixture should look like coarse bread crumbs. Knead in the buttermilk; the mixture will be slightly sticky. Adding more flour will result in a denser biscuit. Place dough on a lightly floured surface. Use a floured rolling pin to roll the dough to ½-inch thickness. Cut out biscuits and place on a baking sheet. Brush the tops of the biscuits with milk and sprinkle with sugar. Bake 14–16 minutes, or until golden brown. Top shortcakes with sweetened strawberries **(recipe page 221)** and whipped cream.

Strawberries for Shortcake

2 pints	Strawberries, cleaned
1 cup	Sugar
1 Tbl	Lemon juice, fresh

Divide the strawberries, purée ½ in the blender, and refrigerate. Slice the other ½ of the strawberries and combine with the sugar and lemon juice. Refrigerate for 2 hours. Add the puréed berries to the sliced berries and serve.

Yield: 8 servings

Pecan Brownies

2 cups	Pecans, chopped
1 cup	Butter
1½ cups	Sugar
½ cup	Brown sugar
½ cup	Chocolate chips, semisweet
2 tsp	Vanilla
4	Eggs
1 cup	Flour
1 cup	Cocoa

Preheat oven to 350 degrees.

In a small sauce pot, place pecans, butter, sugars, and chocolate chips over low heat. Stir constantly until sugars and chocolate melt. Place the mixture in a mixing bowl and add vanilla. Begin beating mixture with an electric mixer. Add eggs 1 at a time. Sift together the flour and cocoa and add it to the rest of the ingredients. Continue to beat on medium speed for 1 minute. Pour batter into a buttered 8 x 12 baking dish. Bake 30–35 minutes.

Yield: 12–16 brownies

Oatmeal Raisin Cookies

½ cup	Butter
½ cup	Crisco shortening
1 cup	Brown sugar
½ cup	Sugar
2	Eggs
2 tsp	Vanilla
1½ cups	Flour
1 tsp	Baking soda
2 tsp	Cinnamon
½ tsp	Salt
3 cups	Oats
1 cup	Golden raisins

Preheat oven to 350 degrees.

Using an electric mixer, beat the butter, shortening, and sugars until creamy. Add eggs 1 at a time. Add vanilla. Combine remaining ingredients together and add them to the creamed butter mixture until everything is mixed well. Drop by rounded spoonfuls onto ungreased baking sheets. Bake for 10–12 minutes. Remove from sheets and place on a cooling rack.

Yield: 18–24 cookies

Cooking Tips

Cookie Dough

A method for making even sized balls of cookie dough is to roll the dough into a cylinder.

Cut the cylinder in half, and each half in half, and so on.

Shortbread Cookies

1 stick	Butter
⅓ cup	Light brown sugar
1 tsp	Vanilla
⅛ tsp	Salt
1¼ cups	Flour
½ cup	Pecans, finely chopped

Preheat oven to 325 degrees.

Using an electric mixer, cream the butter and sugar on slowest speed until light and fluffy. Add the vanilla and salt. Add flour, making sure not to overmix. Fold in pecans by hand. Form dough into 1½-inch diameter balls and place on baking sheet lined with parchment paper. Using the palm of your hand, flatten the dough until it is about ¼ inch thick. Bake 15–18 minutes, just until cookies begin to brown.

Yield: 16–20 cookies

Sugar Cookies

1 cup	Butter
½ cup	Sugar
1 large	Egg
1 Tbl	Vanilla
3 cups	Flour
½ tsp	Baking powder

Preheat oven to 350 degrees.

Cream butter and sugar; beat in egg and vanilla. Sift flour and baking powder together, stir into mixture. Refrigerate about 1 hour, or until dough is firm enough to roll. On a floured surface, roll to ⅛-inch thickness and cut with cookie cutters. Sprinkle the tops with granulated sugar. Bake 10–12 minutes.

Yield: 8 dozen small cookies

Cooking Tips

Coffee Stains

To get coffee stains out of a coffeepot, fill the pot half full of ice cubes, add a few tablespoons of salt and some lemon juice; swish it a few minutes and run it through the dishwasher.

Brown Sugar

For easier storage and measuring of brown sugar, store it in a heavy-duty zipper-lock bag.

A measuring cup will fit inside and it can be packed by pressing the sugar into it through the plastic.

Pralines

1 cup	Heavy cream
2 cups	Brown sugar
1½ cups	Pecans, chopped
4 Tbl	Butter

In a shallow, heavy-duty sauce pot, combine cream and brown sugar. Insert a candy thermometer and cook over medium heat until the mixture reaches 236 degrees. Remove from heat and stir in the pecans. Allow mixture to cool to 110 degrees, stirring occasionally. When mixture has cooled, whip in the butter and continue to whip until the mixture appears light and creamy. Drop by spoonfuls onto wax paper and allow pralines to cool completely before serving.

Yield: 24–30 pralines

Pineapple Sherbet

1 whole	Pineapple, cored and peeled
¾ cup	Sugar
½ cup	Corn syrup
½ cup	Water
1 cup	Milk
1 Tbl	Lemon juice

Mince ¼ of the pineapple and set aside. In a small sauce pot, heat sugar, corn syrup, and water just long enough for the sugar to dissolve. Remove from heat and cool. Place remaining pineapple, sugar syrup, and milk in a blender and purée until smooth. Strain mixture through a colander. Fold in minced pineapple chunks and freeze in an ice-cream maker following the manufacturer's directions. Place frozen mixture in the freezer and allow to sit for 2 hours before serving.

Yield: 6–8 servings

Cooking Tips

Ice-Cream Cones

To prevent ice cream from leaking out of the bottom of a cone, drop in either a mini marshmallow or an inverted Hershey's kiss before the ice cream.

Easter

On Easter Sunday, the Purple Parrot Café will be filled with dozens of hungry families.

Easter is the second busiest lunch shift in the restaurant industry.

Growing up, I spent every Easter at my grandmother's house. Back then, my family never would have thought of eating lunch in a restaurant on such an important holiday. I am glad more people don't think that way today. Families like mine used to be are bad for the restaurant business.

Easter at my grandmother's house always meant leg of lamb. If I were ever afforded the luxury of being able to choose a last meal, my grandmother's leg of lamb would top the list.

Years ago, I would not eat lamb if I thought it was lamb. My mother had to tell me it was roast beef. To pull this off, everyone at the table had to be in on the ruse. "The lamb . . . umm, I mean, the roast beef is good today (wink, wink, nudge, nudge)." To get me to eat turkey, they always told me it was chicken. It is a wonder that to this day, when asked how anything tastes, I don't automatically answer, "Like roast beef . . . or is it like turkey . . . maybe lamb. I don't know, I guess it just tastes like chicken."

As a kid, I would spend the immediate hours after the Easter

sermon surrounded by the huge flowering azaleas in my grandmother's yard. My brother and I trapped bumblebees in washed-out mayonnaise jars that had holes punched in the top. As I sit here today, I can still smell the heady scent of the lamb as it drifted out of the exhaust of the window-unit air conditioners and mixed with the sweet fragrance of all that bloomed in her yard.

For years, I have tried to duplicate my grandmother's leg of lamb, to no avail. It was a simple dish. She didn't use a secret spice combination or complicated roasting procedure. I sat in her kitchen many times and watched her prepare it, but I have never been able to reproduce it.

Maybe what hinders these attempts is that flavor can be replicated, but one can never reproduce a "feel." Those Easter lunches "felt" a certain way. It was a comfortable and safe feeling. I always felt loved in that house. Armed with enough money, I could rebuild her dining room. I still have the table and her china. What I don't have are most of the family members that sat around the table back then. Yes, it is family that is the missing ingredient that gave "feeling" to Easter lunches.

What is left of my extended family rarely eats Sunday lunch together. Some have moved out of state, some have passed on, and some, like me, just can't find the time to host a formal lunch every Sunday. It is unfortunate. I wonder how my grandmother did it. She raised two children as I am doing, yet she cooked and entertained with less effort than anyone I have known.

Eunice Holleman St. John was one of the most kind and gracious ladies who ever lived and ten times the cook I'll ever be. A competent hostess with an overly generous spirit, she was one of the finest

examples of how to live a caring, productive, and fruitful life I ever saw.

I regret that she never had the pleasure of knowing my daughter (her namesake) and my son (her son's namesake), and I wish my children would have had the privilege of knowing her. I would gladly trade all of the busy lunch shifts remaining in my restaurant career for just one more Easter lunch with my grandmother in her house.

Each Easter brings blooming azaleas, flowering dogwoods, and reminiscences of leg-of-lamb lunches spent in the dining room of my grandmother's house. This Easter, I will settle for memories. Memories of family, friends, loved ones, and days long gone. I do, however, look forward to making new memories with my wife and children. I just hope that I can live up to the example that was set for me.

Sides, Extras, and Stuff

Comeback Sauce

Cocktail Sauce

Tartar Sauce

Steak Sauce

Creamy Garlic Salad Dressing

Italian Dressing

1000 Island Dressing

Aunt Tina's Dressing

Mushroom Béchamel Sauce

Pork Stock

Tomato Gravy

Tomato Sauce 1

Tomato Sauce 2 (no meat)

Corn Bread Dressing

Jill's Holiday Cranberry Sauce

Freezer Sandwiches

Pepper Jelly

Louis Norman's
  Garlicky Sweet Dill Pickles

Creole Seasoning

Steak Seasoning

Poultry Seasoning

BBQ Seasoning

Pie Crust 1

Pie Crust 2

Barbara Jane Foote's
  Super Summer Tea

Lemonade

Comeback Sauce

2 cups	Mayonnaise
1 cup	Ketchup
1 cup	Chili sauce
1 cup	Cottonseed oil
1	Large onion, diced
⅓ cup	Lemon juice, freshly squeezed
4 Tbl	Garlic, minced
2 Tbl	Paprika
2 Tbl	Water
2 Tbl	Worcestershire sauce
1 Tbl	Pepper
2 tsp	Dry mustard
2 tsp	Salt

Purée all ingredients in a blender or food processor.
Allow to sit overnight in refrigerator before use.

Yield: 1½ quarts

Squeeze Bottles

To make applying smooth sauces and marinades to foods easier and less messy, use empty pull-top spring water bottles.

There is no brush or bowl to wash and the unused sauce can be refrigerated in the bottle.

Capers

An easy way to remove capers from their tall, narrow jars is to use a vegetable peeler.

The capers line up in the trough of the peeler without rolling out and the liquid drains back into the jar.

Cocktail Sauce

1½ cups	Ketchup
3 Tbl	Fresh lemon juice
2 tsp	Worcestershire sauce
¼ cup	Horseradish, prepared
½ tsp	Black pepper, freshly ground
1½ tsp	Salt

Combine all ingredients and mix well. Refrigerate 2 hours before serving.

Yield: 2 cups

Tartar Sauce

1½ cups	Mayonnaise
¼ cup	Sweet pickle relish
1 Tbl	Yellow mustard
2 Tbl	Capers, chopped
2 Tbl	Green olives, chopped
1½ tsp	Black pepper, freshly ground
1½ tsp	Garlic, minced
½ tsp	Garlic salt
1½ tsp	Parsley
1 Tbl	Lemon juice, freshly squeezed

Combine all ingredients, mix well, and refrigerate 4–6 hours before serving.

Yield: 2½ cups

Peeling Garlic

A quick, easy way to peel garlic is to place the cloves in the center of a rubber jar opener and roll the cloves around inside the soft, thin material.

The paperlike skin of the garlic will slip right off.

Steak Sauce

1 stick	Butter
4 Tbl	Worcestershire sauce
1 Tbl	A.1. Steak Sauce
1 tsp	Liquid Smoke
1 tsp	Hot sauce
2 tsp	**Steak Seasoning (recipe page 253)**

Melt butter over medium-low heat and add remaining ingredients. Stir well and serve with grilled steaks.

Yield: 1 cup

Creamy Garlic Salad Dressing

1 cup	Mayonnaise
⅔ cup	Sour cream
½ cup	Buttermilk
5 tsp	Sugar
2 tsp	Garlic, minced
1¼ tsp	Paprika
1 tsp	Dry mustard
1 tsp	**Creole Seasoning (recipe page 252)**
1 tsp	Salt
2 tsp	Black pepper, freshly ground

Mix thoroughly in a blender until all ingredients are incorporated. Refrigerate and store in an airtight container.

Yield: 2½ cups

Cooking Tips

Storing Garlic

Garlic should be stored in a dry area with good air circulation—never in a plastic bag or Tupperware-style container.

Refrigerated garlic will get soft and moldy.

Garlic in Oil

Peeled garlic in good olive oil and refrigerated will last for a few months.

At room temperature, the garlic will discolor and spoil in a short time.

Italian Dressing

4 cloves	Garlic, minced
½ tsp	Oregano
⅛ tsp	Red pepper flakes
½ cup	White vinegar
1¼ cups	Corn oil
1 Tbl	Sugar
6 Tbl	Water

Place all ingredients in a bottle and shake well. Refrigerate. Make 24 hours in advance of serving. Add 3 ounces feta cheese for a Greek-style dressing.

Yield: 1½ cups

1000 Island Dressing

2 cups	Mayonnaise
½ cup	Chili sauce
2 Tbl	Bell pepper, small dice
1 Tbl	Onion, minced
3 Tbl	Sweet pickle relish
Pinch	Salt
1½	Boiled eggs, chopped

Combine all ingredients thoroughly. Allow to sit overnight in refrigerator before use.

Yield: 3 cups

Perfect Salad Toppings

Use a citrus zester to grate carrots and cucumbers into long, thin strands that are ideal for salads and relishes.

Aunt Tina's Dressing

⅓ cup	Tarragon vinegar
4 Tbl	Apple cider vinegar
2 tsp	Black pepper
1 Tbl	Paprika
2 tsp	Salt
⅓ cup	Blue cheese crumbles
2 tsp	Garlic, minced
1 cup	Canola oil

Place all ingredients together in a glass jar and refrigerate. Shake well before using.

Yield: 1¼ cups

Mushroom Béchamel Sauce

1 Tbl	Olive oil, light
½ cup	Onion, minced
¼ cup	Shallot, minced
¼ cup	Celery, minced
2 tsp	Salt
10 oz	Mushrooms, cleaned and sliced (4 cups)
3 cups	Chicken broth
1 tsp	Garlic, granulated
½ tsp	Thyme, dry
½ cup	Butter
¾ cup	Flour
1 cup	Whipping cream

Heat oil in a 3-quart sauce pot over low heat. Add onions, shallots, celery, and salt. Cook vegetables until tender. Add mushrooms and increase heat to medium. Cook 10 minutes, stirring often. Add chicken broth, garlic, and thyme. Bring back to a simmer and cook 10 more minutes.

In a separate skillet, make a light-blond roux by melting butter and stirring in flour. Add to simmering broth mixture. Cook 3–4 minutes and add cream. Freezes well.

Yield: 2 quarts

Cooking Tips

Re-hydrating Mushrooms

To keep hydrated mushrooms from floating to the top while re-hydrating, place them in a small bowl, covering them with boiling water, and place the grate attachment from your food processor on top of them.

The holes allow water to pass through while keeping the mushrooms submerged.

Separating Fat from Drippings

To separate fat from pan drippings, pour all the liquid from the roasting pan into a glass measuring cup.

Carefully slip a transparent bulb baster beneath the clear layer of fat and pull out the juices into the baster.

Pork Stock

8	Ham hocks
1½ gal	Water
½	Onion

Place hocks, water, and onion in a large stockpot and simmer over low heat eight hours. Add more water as needed to yield 1 gallon of final product. Strain and place stock in refrigerator overnight. Using a large spoon, remove fat layer from top of chilled stock. Stock should be slightly gelatinous. Stock can be frozen in small batches.

Yield: 1 gallon

NOTE:

Reserve ham hock meat for other recipes.

Tomato Gravy

½ cup	Butter
½ cup	Flour
1 cup	Chicken broth, hot
3 large	Tomatoes, ripe, peeled, seeded, and diced, juices reserved
½ cup	Milk
1 tsp	Salt
1 tsp	Black pepper, freshly ground

In a small sauce pot, melt butter over medium heat and stir in flour to make a roux. While roux is cooking, simmer broth and tomatoes together for 2–3 minutes. Slowly whisk broth mixture into the roux. Stir until smooth. Add milk, salt, and pepper. Simmer for 4–5 minutes. Remove from heat and serve.

Yield: 3 cups

Cooking Tips

Peeling Tomatoes

Peel ripe tomatoes by dropping them in boiling water for about 15 to 30 seconds. Remove with a slotted spoon and peel with your fingers.

Tomato Sauce 1

1 lb	Pork, ground
2 cups	Onion, small dice
1½ cups	Carrots, shredded
⅓ cup	Garlic, minced
2 tsp	Basil, dry
1 tsp	Oregano, dry
2	Bay leaves
2 tsp	Salt
2 tsp	Black pepper, freshly ground
6 oz can	Tomato paste
2	28 oz cans tomatoes, diced
1	28 oz can tomatoes, crushed
1½ cups	Water
1 tsp	Balsamic vinegar

In a large heavy-duty sauce pot, brown ground pork over high heat. Drain ½ of the drippings and add onions, carrots, and garlic. Reduce heat and cook vegetables 10 minutes, stirring often to prevent sticking. Add herbs, salt, pepper, and tomato paste and cook 5–6 minutes. (This helps to caramelize the tomato paste, resulting in a sweeter tomato sauce.) Add remaining tomato products and water. Turn heat to low (very low). Allow sauce to cook 3½ hours, stirring occasionally to make sure the sauce doesn't stick. Add vinegar. Sauce is best after 2 or 3 days in the refrigerator. Sauce freezes well.

Yield: 3 quarts

Tomato Sauce 2 (no meat)

¼ cup	Olive oil
2 cups	Onion, small dice
2 cups	Carrots, shredded
⅓ cup	Garlic, minced
2 tsp	Basil, dry
1 tsp	Oregano, dry
2	Bay leaves
2 tsp	Salt
2 tsp	Black pepper, freshly ground
1	6 oz can tomato paste
2	28 oz cans tomatoes, diced
1	28 oz can tomatoes, crushed
1½ cups	Water
1 tsp	Balsamic vinegar

In a large heavy-duty sauce pot, heat olive oil over medium heat. Add onions, carrots, and garlic. Cook vegetables 10 minutes, stirring often. Add herbs, salt, pepper, and tomato paste and cook for 5–6 minutes. (This helps to caramelize the tomato paste, resulting in a sweeter tomato sauce.) Add remaining tomato products and water. Turn heat to low (very low). Allow sauce to cook for 3½ hours, stirring often. Add vinegar. Sauce is best after 2 or 3 days in the refrigerator. Sauce freezes well.

Yield: 3 quarts

Cooking Tips

Stained Tupperware

Spray Tupperware with nonstick cooking spray before pouring in tomato based sauces, to avoid staining.

Corn Bread Dressing

1	Cornish (game) hen
2 quarts	Chicken broth
½	Onion
½	Carrot
1	Bay leaf
1 Tbl	Bacon grease (or canola oil)
¼ cup	Bell pepper, diced
1 cup	Celery, diced
1 cup	Onion, diced
2 tsp	Celery salt
2 tsp	**Poultry Seasoning (recipe page 254)**
2 cups	**Mushroom Béchamel Sauce (recipe page 241)**
2 cups	Heavy cream
1½ cups	Chicken broth, strained from cooking hen
4	Eggs
2	Eggs, hard-boiled
1 recipe	**Basic Corn Bread, crumbled (recipe page 201)**

Place the hen, broth, onion, carrot, and bay leaf in medium stockpot. Simmer 1 hour and 20 minutes over medium heat. Remove hen and strain the broth. Allow hen to cool and pull meat from the bones. Chop meat.

Preheat oven to 325 degrees.

In a medium skillet, melt bacon grease over low heat. Add vegetables and seasoning and cook slowly for 10 minutes. Pour into a mixing bowl. Add mushroom béchamel sauce, cream, broth, and eggs, mixing well. Add crumbled corn bread and hen meat. Mix until all is well incorporated. Pour into a 3-quart baking dish. Bake 1 hour and 15 minutes. Do not overcook dressing (it should be moist but not runny).

Yield: 8–12 servings

Loaf Pan Liner

When lining a loaf pan with plastic wrap to make a frozen mousse, sprinkle the pan with water first.

Water droplets cause the plastic wrap to cling smoothly to the metal without bunching or forming large air pockets.

Jill's Holiday Cranberry Sauce

12 oz bag	Fresh cranberries
1 cup	Port wine
½ cup	White sugar
½ cup	Brown sugar
½ cup	Orange juice
2 tsp	Cornstarch
2 Tbl	Cold water

Combine cranberries, port, sugars, and orange juice in a sauté pan and simmer over medium heat for 20–30 minutes or until the cranberries become soft. Separately, mix the cornstarch with the cold water, then add it to the cranberry mixture. Turn up heat to a heavy simmer and continue to cook, stirring well, for another 5–10 minutes. Serve warm.

Yield: 3 cups

Freezer Sandwiches

1 stick	Butter, melted
3 Tbl	Prepared horseradish
3 Tbl	Dijon mustard
2 Tbl	Poppy seeds
8	Hamburger buns
1 lb	Ham, thinly sliced
8 slices	Swiss cheese

Combine butter, horseradish, mustard, and poppy seeds. Mix thoroughly. Open hamburger buns and brush both sides of the inside with the poppy seed dressing. Place 2 ounces of ham and 1 slice of cheese on bottom part of bun. Repeat with the remainder of the buns. Close the tops of the buns and brush more of the poppy seed dressing on the outside tops and bottoms of buns. Tightly wrap each sandwich in aluminum foil and freeze.

To cook, preheat oven to 400 degrees. Place sandwich, still tightly wrapped in foil, directly on the center rack for approximately 30–45 minutes until center is hot and cheese is melted.

Yield: 8 sandwiches

Polenta

To avoid lumpy
polenta, pour
cornmeal into a metal
colander, tapping it
gently so that the
meal falls slowly,
steadily, and evenly
into boiling water.

Pepper Jelly

4 large	Bell peppers, seeds removed
8	Jalapeños, seeds removed
1	Red pepper, seeds removed
6½ cups	Sugar
1½ cups	White vinegar
6 oz	Liquid pectin

Place peppers in a food processor and pulse into large, rough-chopped pieces. Place the sugar, vinegar, and peppers in a nonreactive sauce pot. Bring to a simmer and cook for 12 minutes. Add pectin and return to a simmer. Cook another 5 minutes. Remove from heat and pour jelly into canning jars. Top with lids and place jars in a water bath. Boil for 10 minutes.

Yield: 1 quart

Louis Norman's Garlicky Sweet Dill Pickles

Start with 1 gallon of the cheapest dill pickles you can find. (Do not use kosher dills.) Drain and discard all the juice and cut pickles into 1-inch segments. Next, layer approximately 2 inches of pickle segments back into the bottom of the empty 1-gallon pickle jar. Top pickles with approximately 2 teaspoons of minced garlic and pour enough granulated sugar over the top of the pickles to cover (approximately 1–1½ cups). Repeat procedure until you have filled the pickle jar. Close lid tightly and let sit. Within 6 hours, the sugar will dissolve and make a new, sweeter pickle liquid. Add an additional cup (or 2) of sugar, making sure that the pickles are always covered by sugar or liquid.

Store pickles in the refrigerator for 3 days. Rotate the jar twice a day to thoroughly mix ingredients.

This is not a pickling recipe. True canners will scoff at this procedure, since raw cucumbers aren't being used. But who cares what they think? The end result is worth the loss of authenticity. The hardest part of the recipe is finding plain-old dill pickles. Kosher dills won't work (they shrivel up). Louis slices his garlic into small chips (about 2 heads per gallon of pickles). I use minced garlic.

Garlic Breath
Chewing 3 or 4 sprigs of fresh parsley is the best remedy for garlic breath.

Creole Seasoning

½ cup	Lawry's Seasoned Salt
2 Tbl	Onion powder
2 Tbl	Paprika
1 Tbl	Cayenne pepper
1 Tbl	White pepper
1 Tbl	
plus 1 tsp	Garlic powder
1 Tbl	Black pepper
1 tsp	Dry mustard
1 tsp	Oregano, dry
1 tsp	Thyme, dry

Combine all ingredients and mix well. Store in an airtight container.

Yield: 1 cup

Steak Seasoning

½ cup	Lawry's Seasoned Salt
⅓ cup	Black pepper
¼ cup	Lemon pepper
2 Tbl	Garlic salt
2 Tbl	Granulated garlic
1 Tbl	Onion powder

Combine all ingredients and mix well. Store in an airtight container.

Yield: 1⅓ cups

Poultry Seasoning

¼ cup	Lawry's Seasoned Salt
¼ cup	Garlic powder
¼ cup	White pepper
¼ cup	Lemon pepper
¼ cup	Celery salt

Combine and mix well. Store in an airtight container.

Yield: 1¼ cups

BBQ Seasoning

⅓ cup	Lawry's Seasoned Salt
⅓ cup	Paprika
2 Tbl	Onion powder
2 Tbl	Cayenne pepper
1 Tbl	White pepper
5 tsp	Garlic powder
1 Tbl	Black pepper
1 Tbl	Dry mustard
1 tsp	Oregano
1 tsp	Thyme

Mix thoroughly.

Yield: 1 cup

Rolling Pin

A chilled, unopened bottle of white wine with straight sides (sauvignon blanc) is perfect for use as a makeshift rolling pin.

The weight is good and the cold temperature is good for rolling pie dough.

Pie Crust 1

2 cups	Flour, all-purpose
1 cup	Crisco shortening
¼ tsp	Salt
1	Egg
⅓ cup	Milk

Blend the first 3 ingredients together with a pastry cutter or a fork. Beat egg and milk together. Slowly add egg/milk mixture to flour mixture, 1 tablespoon at a time, until pie dough becomes moist and forms a ball. Divide into 2 equal parts and shape each half into a ball. Wrap and refrigerate one hour before rolling. Roll out on a floured surface.

Yield: 2 crusts

To roll out dough: Remove dough disk from refrigerator. If stiff and very cold, let stand until dough is cool but malleable.

Using a floured rolling pin, roll dough disk on a lightly floured surface from the center out in each direction, forming a 12-inch circle. To transfer dough, carefully roll it around the rolling pin, lift, and unroll dough, centering it in an ungreased 9-inch pie plate.

Pie Crust 2

1⅓ cups	Flour, all-purpose
½ tsp	Salt
½ cup	Crisco shortening
3 Tbl	Ice water

Mix flour and salt in mixing bowl. Cut shortening into the flour with a pastry cutter, until mixture resembles the texture of tiny peas. Do not use your hands, as the heat from your hands will melt the shortening, causing the pastry to be heavy, not light and flaky.

Add ice water and combine with a fork. It may appear as if it needs more water; it does not. Quickly gather the dough into a ball and flatten into a 4-inch-wide disk. Wrap in plastic and refrigerate for 30–45 minutes.

Yield: 1 crust

To roll out dough: Remove dough disk from refrigerator. If stiff and very cold, let stand until dough is cool but malleable.

Using a floured rolling pin, roll dough disk on a lightly floured surface from the center out in each direction, forming a 12-inch circle. To transfer dough, carefully roll it around the rolling pin, lift, and unroll dough, centering it in an ungreased 9-inch pie plate.

Cooking Tips

Freezing Pie Pastry

In order to streamline the process of baking pies, prepare several batches of dough at once, roll them out between sheets of plastic wrap, stack the disks in a pizza box, and keep the box in the freezer.

Tea Bag Removal

For easier tea bag removal from hot water, tie tea bag strings together, then slide a skewer through them.

Position the skewer across the top of the boiler or pitcher with the tea bags dangling in the water.

When the tea is finished brewing, simply remove the skewer.

Barbara Jane Foote's Super Summer Tea

2 qts	Boiling water
6	Tea bags (regular size, or 3 family size)
Handful	Fresh mint
¼ tsp	Cinnamon
⅛ tsp	Ground cloves 1½ cups
Sugar	
6 oz can	Frozen orange juice concentrate
6 oz can	Frozen lemonade concentrate
6 oz can	Pineapple juice
	Mint

Pour boiling water over tea, mint, cinnamon, and cloves. Steep for 20 minutes. Strain into a 1-gallon pitcher. Add sugar, stir until dissolved. Add juices and stir well. Fill pitcher with ice. Can be served hot or cold.

Yield: 3 quarts

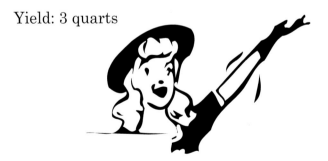

Lemonade

1½ cups	Sugar
1½ cups	Water, boiling
3½ cups	Water, ice cold
1 cup	Lemon juice, fresh
	(approximately 12–14 lemons for juicing)
1	Lemon, thinly sliced into rounds
1 sprig	Mint

Combine sugar and boiling water and mix until all sugar is dissolved. Add ice water and lemon juice and stir well. Add lemon slices and serve chilled. Fresh mint adds a nice cool flavor.

Yield: 2 quarts

Index